Reflections of Contemporary Irish Men

Reflections of Contemporary Irish Men

by Valerie O'Sullivan

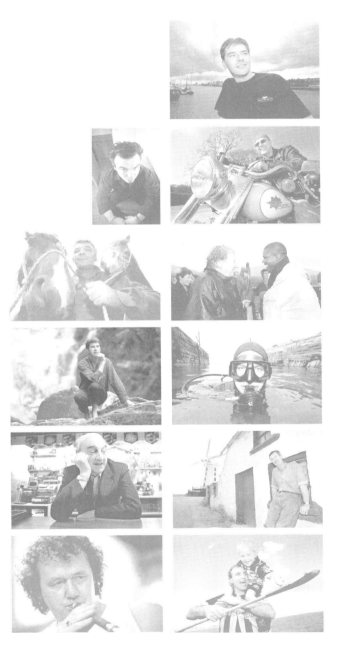

VERITAS

Published 2000 by
Veritas Publications
7/8 Lower Abbey Street
Dublin I

ISBN 1 85390 526 7

Acknowledgements
The author would like to thank the following people for their help and support:
Ger O'Sullivan of IT Support, Doreen O'Doherty of Murphy Print, Killarney;
Pat Moore from Irremore, County Kerry;
Colette Dower, Toner Quinn and all the staff at Veritas Publications;
To all my family and circle of bawdy friends, your support and encouragement will always be
appreciated.

'Advent' and the excerpts from 'A Christmas Childhood' and 'Ploughman' by Patrick
Kavanagh are reprinted with the permission of the Trustees of the Estate of the late
Katherine B. Kavanagh, through the Jonathan Williams Literary Agency. 'A Thought From
Hildegard' by Pádraig J. Daly from *The Voice of the Hare* (The Dedalus Press, 1997) is
reprinted with the permission of the publisher. 'Sea Fever' by John Masefield is reprinted
with the permission of The Society of Authors as the literary representative of the Estate of
John Masefield. 'If' by Rudyard Kipling is reprinted with the permission of A P Watt Ltd on
behalf of The National Trust for Places of Historical Interest or Historical Beauty. The
translation of Caitlín Maude's poem 'Impí' is reprinted with the permission of Gabriel
Fitzmaurice. 'To Do What is Good with My Life' from *The Calm Beneath the Storm* (Veritas,
1983) is reprinted with the permission of Donal Neary SJ. The excerpt from 'The Dry
Salvages' by T. S. Eliot from *The Four Quartets* in *Collected Poems 1909-1962* is reprinted with
the permission of Faber and Faber.

Designed by Bill Bolger and Valerie O'Sullivan
Printed by Betaprint Ltd, Dublin

Contributors

Preface

The pictures and reflections for this book started with Mickey Ned O'Sullivan on a cold but beautiful Kerry day in the Dromoughty Valley, near Kenmare. From there, through negotiating the Irish landscape, and weaving through many roads in my spare time, I met people who allowed the landscape that they have grown to love to speak through them.

From the beginning the book took on a life of its own. Visiting these men, in their chosen place, allowed me to show that the sensitivities that we attribute to women also find a deep echo in men's lives. Through the poems and prayers chosen, through the thoughts expressed, these men speak honestly, uninhibited and unashamed. Their diversity of life and the very nature of their work speaks for itself. Their love for family, their sense of place, the joys and sorrows, the total devastation felt after losing a loved one, these admissions are all included.

The men have drawn their reflections from life as it has unfolded around them. In their gentle and caring way, I feel these men are beckoning and encouraging those about them to a better future. Each one of the contributors has a wonderful story to tell, whether it involves composing music, manning Carrestoona Cross, opening the Shannon lock, playing hurling for your county, selling horses, writing for a newspaper, entertaining audiences, farming, changing Government law, making accordions, teaching, driving motorbikes, construction, or pastoral and parish work.

The recurrence of Patrick Kavanagh's work is significant, as are the lines from Kahlil Gibran's *The Prophet*:

Is not religion all deeds and all reflection,
And that which is neither deed nor reflection, but a wonder and a surprise ever springing in the soul,
even while the hands hew the stone or tend the loom?
Who can separate his faith from his actions, or his belief from his occupations?

Valerie O'Sullivan

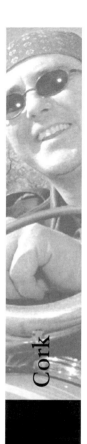

Cork

Bobby Hilliard

Bobby Hilliard is a master plasterer and developer in Cork City. He specialises in the restoration of old stone houses, most notably some of the recent restorations of buildings in Barrick Street at the heart of the city. Married to Maria Skedeack from Sweden, they have two sons, Robert and Johnaton, and with their two Harley-Davidson bikes the family love to head to west Cork for weekends. Bobby also enjoys Tae Kwon Do, watching boxing and, of course, restoring old houses. His parents Phil and Joe Hilliard also live in Cork.

'During the course of our history, for such a small country in terms of size and population, the Irish race has produced some fine leaders, writers, athletes, singers, songwriters, dancers, and actors. In all walks of life, their will to win, be seen, heard and succeed has always impressed me. I hope this new millennium will bring forward that same desire, and that the Irish people will remain true to themselves and their own individuality.'

Bobby Hilliard heading off to work on his Harley-Davidson

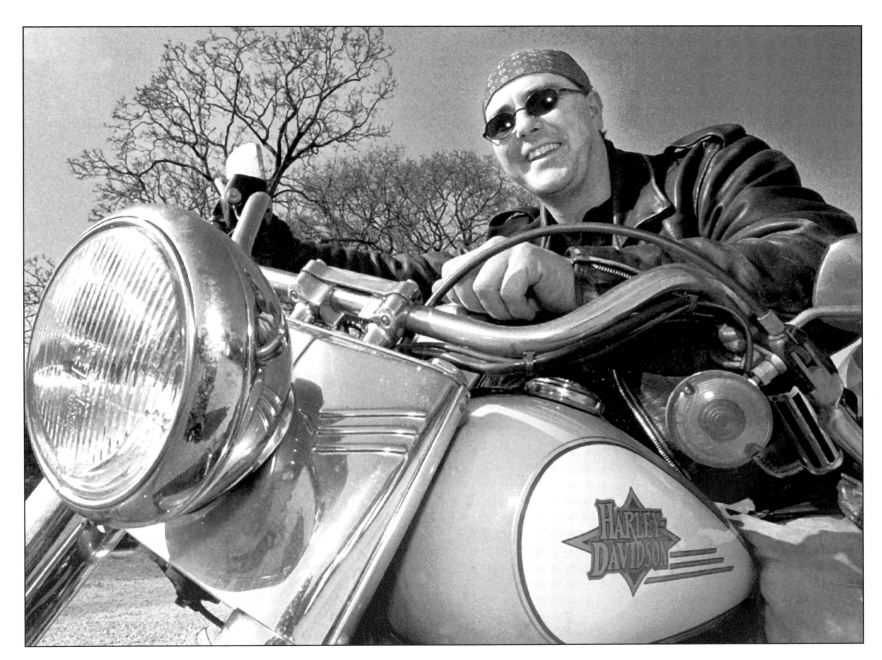

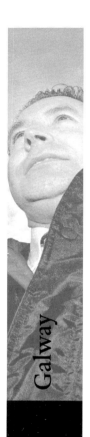

Galway

Brian Conway

Brian Conway is a native of Ballyhaunis, County Mayo. He studied electronic engineering in Galway and then undertook further studies in business with the Irish Management Institute, carving out a career in public relations and event management with Nortel Networks Ireland.

Brian became involved in the Royal National Lifeboat Institution in the early 1990s and was one of four founding members of Galway Lifeboat station, which was put on service on 27 March 1996. He is Station Administration Officer (SAO) for Galway Lifeboat, and a former treasurer and founder member of the National Maritime Ball, which raises funds for Irish Lifeboats. Brian is also a member of the Galway Junior Chamber of Commerce and of the Galway Bay Sailing Club.

'The RNLI was founded in 1824 by Sir William Hillary who was a lifeboat man himself. The RNLI celebrated its 175th anniversary of saving lives at sea in 1999 and is held in the highest regard in international lifeboat circles. Many lifeboat services throughout the world have modelled themselves on the institution, its lifeboats, equipment and expertise.

While the RNLI has been supported entirely by voluntary contributions, the highest standards of professionalism have been maintained in every sphere of its activities. The enormous amount of personal dedication and commitment given by all of the lifeboat crew in Galway, indeed, throughout the country, knows no bounds. They all display immense courage and without any doubt all are heroes. On every call, be it day or night, no matter what the conditions, the crews risk their lives to save people in distress at sea, seeking no glory or reward.

Since first going on station in 1996, Galway Lifeboat has launched 112 times and saved 49 lives in Galway. I am proud to be part of this voluntary honourable organisation. All of the volunteers, be they crew, fund-raisers or supporters, share a unique combination of being the most genuinely committed people. It is they who are the strength behind the continuing success story that is Irish Lifeboats.'

'With Courage…everything is possible'

Sir William Hillary, founder of the RNLI

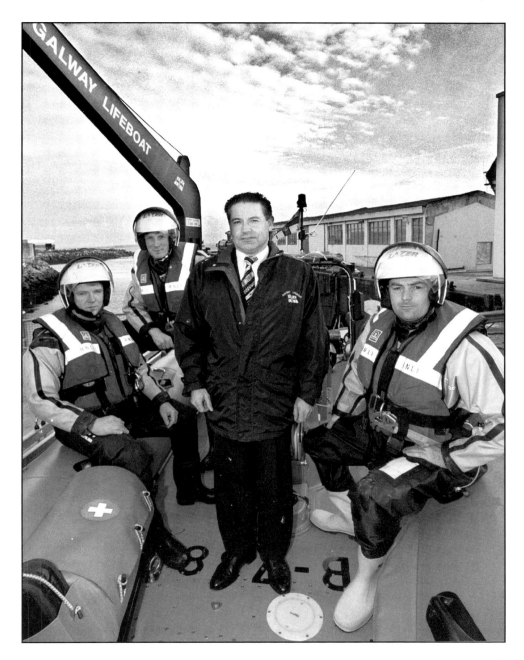

'Wouldst thou'– so the helmsman answered
'Learn the secret of the sea?
Only those who brave its dangers
comprehend its mystery!'

from *The Galley of Count Arnaldos*
by Henry Wadsworth Longfellow (1807–82)

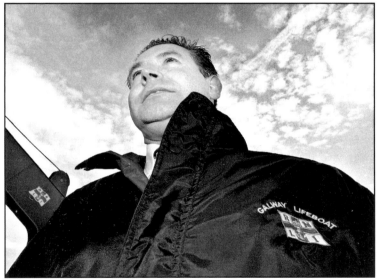

Brian Conway pictured with crewmen from the RNLI boat in Galway Bay – Mike Swan, Robert Goodbody and John McGrath.

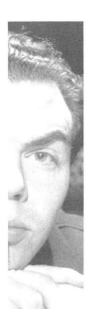

Jack Lukeman has been declared as Ireland's first superstar of the millennium by *Hot Press* magazine. His album *Metropolis Blue* reached platinum status, consisting entirely of original material written in conjunction with David Constantine. Jack's voice has been compared to, and inspired by, amongst others, Scott Walker, Frank Sinatra and Jim Morrison. As well as his huge appeal in Ireland, he has played to audiences in New York, London, Paris, Germany and Brussels.

Originally from Athy, County Kildare, Jack is 26 years old. His former apprenticeship as a mechanic allowed him to perfect his vocal technique...when the garage was empty! In the quiet, he would fill the space with his haunting voice. Songs from his bestselling album include 'Georgie Boy', 'When the Moon is High', 'I ain't crazy', 'Metropolis Blue', and 'Ode to the Ed Wood'.

It's the little things that make this life
so beautiful, so glorious, so divine,
like a summer breeze on a warm July night.
Makes me wanna kiss the stars
as they shine in your smile.

from *When The Moon Is High* by Jack Lukeman and David Constantine

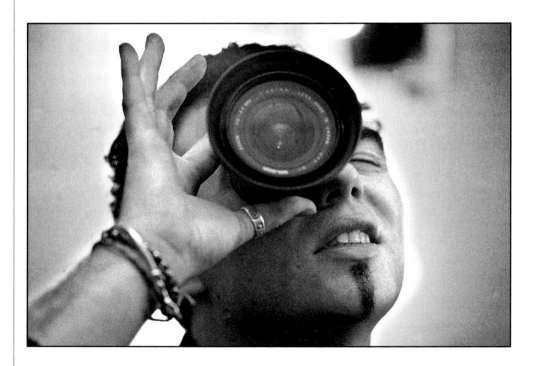

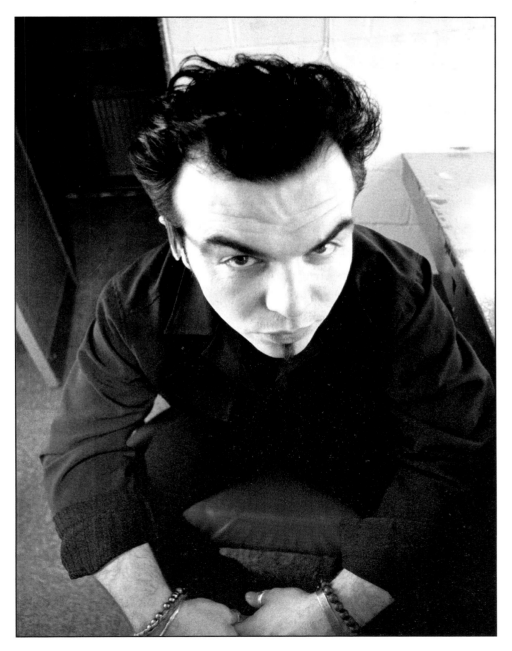

Rooftop Lullaby

Mother is there something in the sky?
Something up there that they hide?
A jewel for me and you, apple trees
with fallen fruit?
Daughter now I don't know but I believe
That its beauty's beyond words.
It's like a tune that I can't sing
But I've heard it sung by birds.
It's a rooftop lullaby
Fallen from the sky
Sends us to sleep tonight.
It's the apple in your eye
Keeps you as sweet as pie
Dreaming through the night.
Father won't you tell me if you know.
Where does half of the moon go?
When it's not up in the sky
It disappears before my eyes.
Oh my son why does the morning break each day?
Why do people pass away?
Oh it's the mystery and truth
It's the innocence in youth
A rooftop lullaby
Fallen from the sky
Sends us to sleep tonight.
It's the apple in your eye
Keeps you as sweet as pie
Dreaming through the night.
A rooftop lullaby
Fallen from the sky
Send us to sleep tonight.

from the album *Metropolis Blue* (1999)

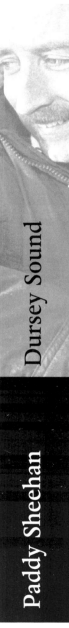

Paddy Sheehan is the cable-car operator at Dursey Sound. He operates a service to Dursey Island, which is situated off the Beara Penninsula. The service to the Island goes twice daily. There are now just eight people living on the island and the cable car is a valuable service, transporting farm animals and livestock to the island. Paddy lives nearby with his wife Agnes and two children Madeleine and Damien. They run a bed and breakfast and coffee shop in the summer time. In 1995, Paddy was Home Maker of the Year in west Cork. Paddy enjoys rock fishing, hill walking and is a member of the Allihies liturgy group and church maintenance committee.

The Sea Flower

'In memory of my brother John Michael Sheehan and the crew of *The Sea Flower*. On 22 December 1968 – a stormy night – their boat capsized in appalling weather conditions. All five fishermen were drowned: my brother, our first cousin Noel Sheehan from Dursey Island, skipper Michael Crowley from Bere Island, Bernie Lynch from Bere Island and Niall Crilly from Cork City. The raging seas kept her back from entering Bantry Bay, and it went on the rocks near Ardgroom at Kenmare Bay.

While the wild winds blew
and the helpless crew
spent all that long night signalling to the shore,
the storm raged and they thought of home
and their loved ones left behind.

Paddy Sheehan

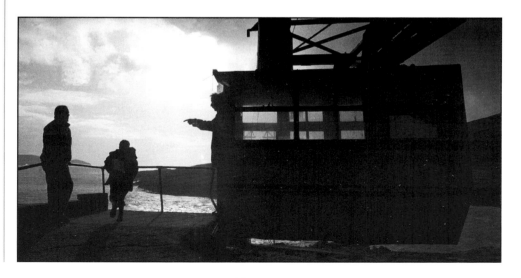

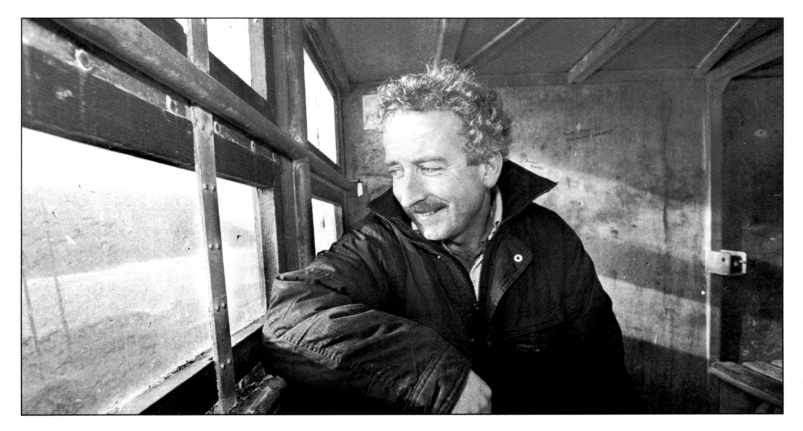

I would like to remember the late Paddy Urhan, skipper of the *Ard Beara*, Denis O'Driscoll, Denis Lowney and Richie Daly, all of whom went in aid of *The Sea Flower*. Despite their valiant efforts, they were unable to rescue the crew. She had already broken up on the rocks.

My father David Strack and John Micheal fished together around Dursey Island in a small wooden boat driven with a small seagull engine. They fished the old lobster-pot and braved the strong tides. My mother Josephine Dwyer worked hard on the farm, saving the hay and baking the home-made bread. She would pray for their safe return from sea; she was a wonderful mother.'

'Every day on Dursey, the island people see the last sunset in Europe.'

Bless them O Lord and be with us we pray.
May all that we do be done in your name.
Lord, keep them together up there in your Heaven.
Amen

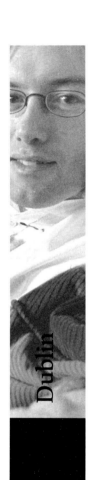

Dublin

Michael Flynn

Michael Flynn is a founder member of The Café Orchestra, a four-piece band formed in Dublin in 1991 who play their own blend of café jazz and gypsy music. Michael has played the piano accordion since childhood and has developed his own unique style of playing. The band has performed at the Burgen Blues Festival, the Cannes Film Festival, and made appearances in the movie *Michael Collins* and Brendan O'Carroll's *Agnes Browne*. As well as regular concerts, The Café Orchestra has played for Maureen O'Hara's seventieth birthday, for Martin Scorcese, and for Gregory Peck. They have produced four albums to date: *Topáz*, *After Hours*, *Feel Good* and *Trés Café*.

Michael is a native of Goatstown, County Dublin, and is the son of Michael and Nancy Flynn. He enjoys swimming, diving and poetry, is a devoted Elvis fan, and has a love of nature as well as a fascination with the seasons of the year.

A little rant-and-rave:

'This high-speed, DVD, USB, MP3, text-message, 'dot ie' world in which we live can get a little confusing...can't it? Sometimes we lose sight of the essentials, spending hours of anguish over what flavour computer should we buy, how the property market will make or break us, and whether or not a certain foreign football team will do the double next year. It's easy to feel caught, lost, disillusioned, and disconnected.

Well, listen up: simplify the equation...

You always have a choice, there is always another way and nothing is impossible. Listen to the music in the voice of someone you love, the waves on the beach, watch the morning sun, the neons against a cloudy city sky – all food for the soul, and not a penny gained or lost. I say hey, take a chance, dream the dream, live life, give your love unconditionally and value the friendships you make, and no matter what the hell happens, don't worry! In a hundred years from now it won't matter a whole lot anyway! This is not a thought for the day. It is a thought for everyday.

Who am I to say? I'm just a man who plays the squeeze-box for a living, and by virtue of that insanity am probably just as qualified as anyone else to state the bloody obvious. Am I a "Contemporary Irish Man"? In this era, where time is money, I'd prefer to be timeless.'

14

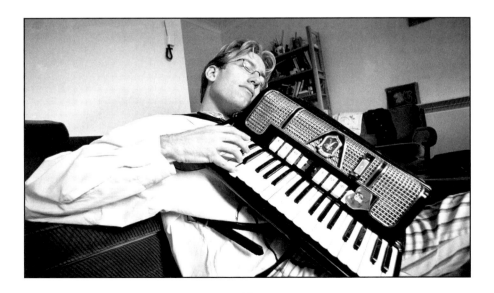

Do not break
the clear glass
between us
　　　(no glass is broken
　　　without blood and pain)
for beyond is Heaven
or beyond is Hell
and what good is Heaven
if it is not
for ever? –
the loss of
Heaven
is the worst Hell…

from 'Impí' [Entreaty]
by Caitlín Maude (1941-82),
translated by Gabriel Fitzmaurice

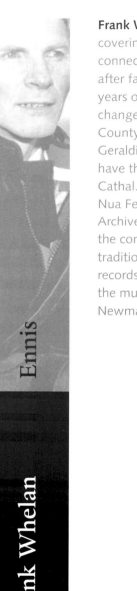

Ennis

Frank Whelan

Frank Whelan is a techician/supervisor covering County Clare with the ESB, connecting new houses, and looking after faults in all weather. With thirty years of service he has seen many changes. Frank is a native of Shragh, County Clare, and is married to Geraldine Whelan from Adelaide. They have three children, Eoin, Brendan and Cathal. Frank is chairman of The Fleadh Nua Festival and head of the Traditional Archive in Cois na hAbhna. He plays the concert flute, has a love for traditional music, and collects and records the music of Clare, especially the music of Paddy O'Donoghue from Newmarket-on-Fergus.

'When rural electrification came to our area in west Clare, a new sense of hope came with it. The radio brought famous musicians and singers into our house, and the stories of ghosts and fairies soon faded away to be replaced by long discussions on the heroes of football, hurling and music. Gone were the lonesome shadows made of the old oil lamp and the distinct hiss of tilly lamp.

My childhood winter nights were filled with music and song and listening to the old men tracing various deeds through history; so vivid were their descriptions that I felt I had lived then.

All of us have the responsibility to ensure that this precious heritage, so selflessly given to us, is passed on to the next generation.'

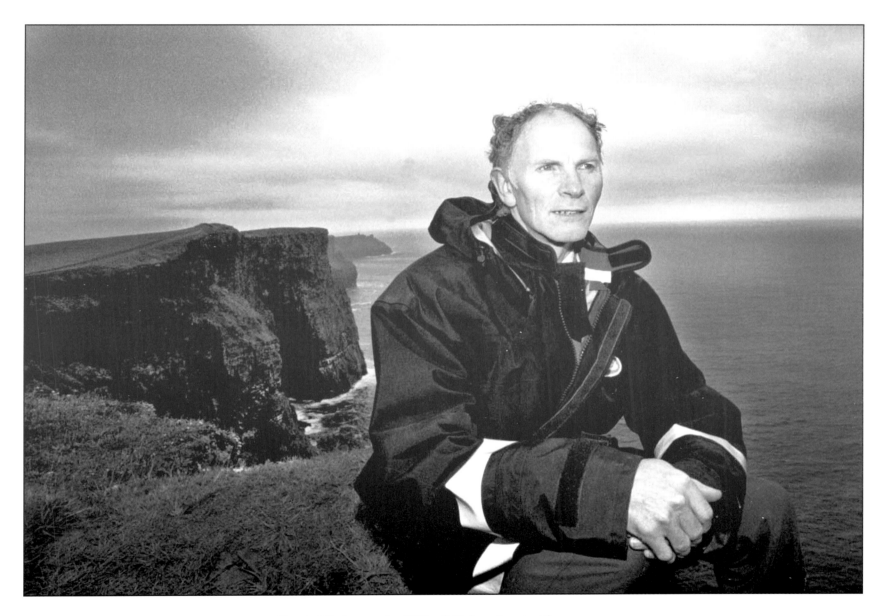

Frank Whelan on the Cliffs of Moher, County Clare

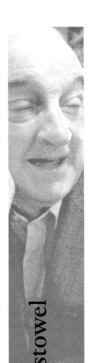

Listowel

John B. Keane

John B. Keane is one of Ireland's best known authors. His first play *Sive*, produced in 1959 by Listowel Drama Group, was an instant hit, and since then he has written nineteen plays, which have been performed all over the world. He was born in Listowel in 1928 and started his career as a pharmaceutical chemist. In 1955, John B. bought his famous public house in Listowel. Some of his best-known plays include *Sharon's Grave, Many Young Men of Twenty, The Year of the Hiker, Big Maggie, Moll,* and of course his most famous play *The Field*, which was brought to the screen by Noel Pearson and Jim Sheridan in 1991. His novels include *The Bodhrán Makers* and *Durango* and he has written numerous essays, short stories, and his celebrated *Letters* series.

John B. is married to Mary O'Connor and their family include Billy, Conor, John and Johanna, and two grand-daughters, Anne and Laura. John B. is President of Writers Week in Listowel, President of PEN (an international association of writers) in Ireland, and is a member of Aosdána. He was awarded honorary doctorates from Trinity College, Dublin, and Marymount Manhattan College, New York. He enjoys walking, reading, occasional beer drinking, and sport – particularly gaelic football, hurling and rugby.

'For all travellers, myself included, wherever or whoever they may be, please change those of evil intent to good.

We're all travellers anyway...'

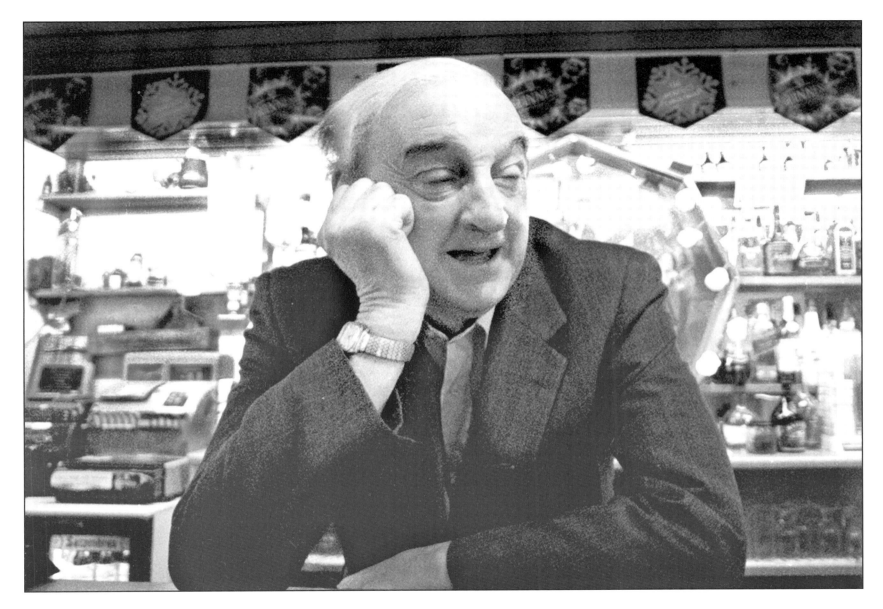

John B. Keane enjoying the banter with locals as he makes a rare visit back to his pub in the heart of Listowel town, north Kerry

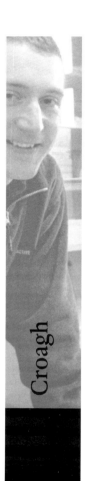

Croagh

Niall West

Niall West is a teacher at Rathkeale No.2 National School, County Limerick, which is under Church of Ireland management. The school has seventeen pupils and Niall teaches third to sixth classes. Originally from nearby Croagh, he is a former pupil of the Church of Ireland school in Adare, County Limerick, where his mother Joan taught. His grandmother Kathleen Shier was also a teacher there. Niall plays badminton and enjoys reading and travel. Before returning to his native Croagh in 1999 he taught in Kilcommon National School in County Wicklow for nine years.

'You never know what life is going to throw at you. Be prepared for whatever happens and always be ready to accept what happens in your life.'

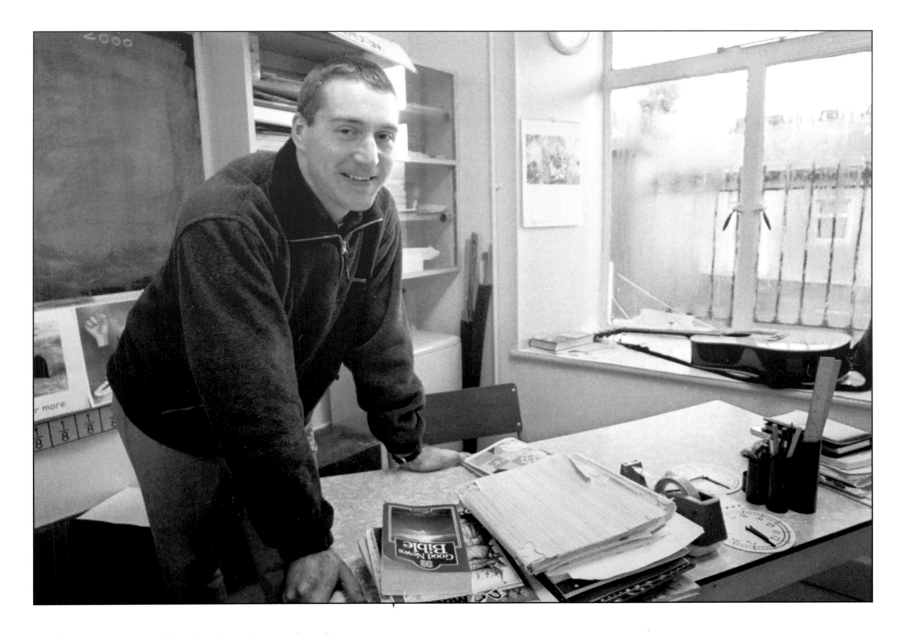

Niall West carries on a long family tradition of teaching

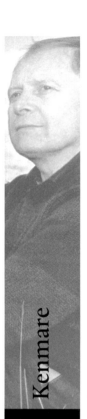

Kenmare

Michael O'Sullivan

Michael (Mickey Ned) O'Sullivan is a native of Kenmare, County Kerry. A member of the glorious Kerry football team of 1970–1980, and captain in 1975, he was manager of the team from 1989 until 1992. Michael teaches in Coláiste Gobnatan, Baile Mhuirne, County Cork, teaching geography, physical education, career guidance and religion. He is married to Marian O'Sullivan (née King) from Currow and they have two sons, Brian and Eamon. Both Marian and Michael run a coffee shop in Kenmare town and are avid hillwalkers who enjoy all outdoor activities.

'Living in such a beautiful area as Kenmare, I see a great need to preserve the beauty of the landscape and the environment, and not to spoil it for future generations by indiscriminate planning. Small rural settlements provide great advantages for family life, and yet there are economic and social factors contributing to rural depopulation that are disturbing. There is a great need for both the government and local communities to combine to address this problem. I think that there is a lack of overall balance in the perceived priorities of contemporary society in Ireland. There seems to be too much emphasis placed on the relentless pursuit of materialistic values. Happiness is perceived solely as satisfying one's personal desires. Man has always pursued happiness, but nowadays, because of social pressures, etc., it is becoming increasingly more difficult for people to know how to pursue it.

From an educational point of view, I think young people need help in identifying priorities in life. Happiness has a number of basic ingredients, health being the most important one, but it is further enhanced by an ability to develop and nurture good family relationships and friendships. Another aspect is being able to appreciate beauty in nature and art, having an expression of oneself through one's interests. Contrary to modern perceptions, all that is required is a reasonable standard of living, and an ability to pursue an inner meaning to life in order to make sense of it all.

Young people need to learn that it is not what one has, and what one wants, that makes them happy, but what they are and what they become. These basic values are best achieved within the family. Happiness is there for the taking...it's up to each individual to find it.'

Michael is pictured in the Dromoughty valley overlooking Kenmare Bay, County Kerry

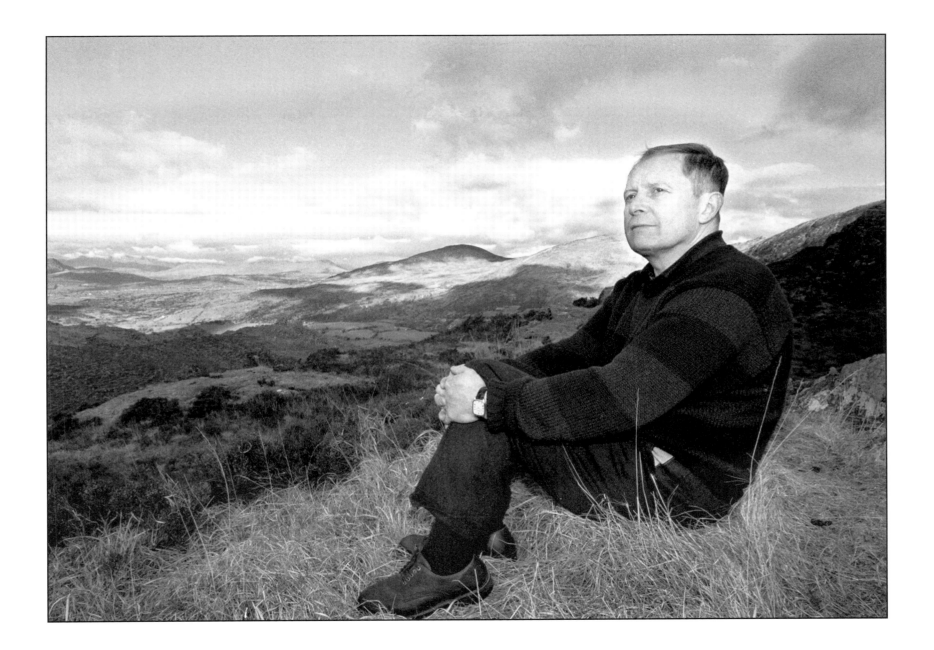

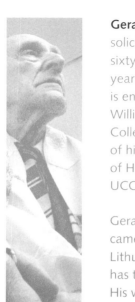

Gerald Y. Goldberg Cork

Gerald Yule Goldberg is a retired solicitor in Cork where he practiced for sixty-five years. Now, at eighty-eight years of age, with a doctorate in law, he is engaged in writing a thesis on William Shakespeare at University College Cork. He has presented much of his James Joyce library and collection of Hebrew and Jewish books to the UCC Library.

Gerald is a native of Cork. His parents came in to the Port of Cork from Lithuania on their way to America. He has three sons, John, Theo and David. His wife Sheila passed away in 1998. Gerald was a Fianna Fáil Councillor with Cork Corporation for twenty years, and was Lord Mayor of Cork in 1977. He is Chairman of the Cork Orchestral Society and a committee member of Cork Opera House. He has a great love of music and literature, but what is most important to him is friendship.

'How strange it is that before a young law student may be entered into practice, either as a solicitor or barrister, he must qualify in a branch of law known as equity. Equity contains a number of rules, among which is this: "He who comes into equity must come with clean hands." When as a law student I reached the subject of equity I shuddered with delight, for there before me was a teaching that every orthodox Jewish youth learns at an early age. But first consider the teaching of the 24th psalm:

The earth is the Lord's, and the fullness thereof;
the world, and they that dwell therein.
For it is He that hath founded it upon the seas,
And establishes it upon the floods.

The foregoing is part of the morning prayers of all males, and they must remember the rules and obligations that every day of their lives are thrust upon them. This then is one:

These are the things, the fruits of which a man enjoys in this world while the stock remains for him for the world to come, viz, honouring father and mother, the practice of charity, timely attendance at the house of study morning and evening, hospitality to any wayfarers, visiting the sick, dowrying the bride, attending the dead to the grave, devotion in prayer, and making peace between man and his fellow; but the study of the law leadeth to them all.

And then comes this magnificent anticipation of the rule of equity:

Who may ascend the mountain of the Lord?
And who may stand in His holy place?
He that hath clean hands, and a pure heart;
Who hath not set his desire upon vanity
And hath not sworn deceitfully.
He shall receive a blessing from the Lord,
And righteousness from the God of his salvation.

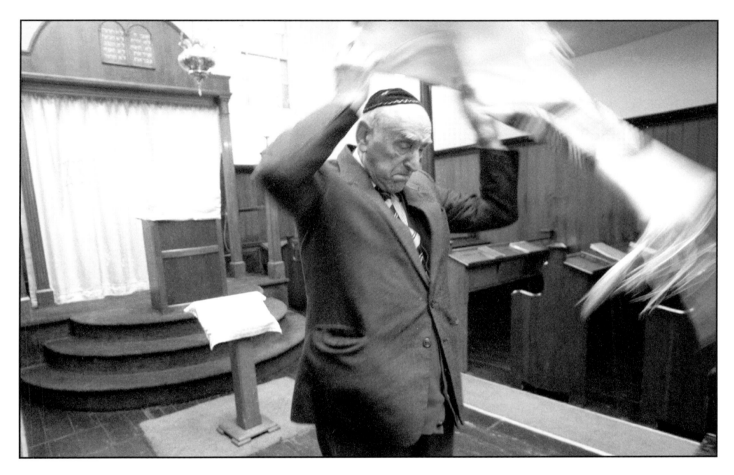

When I was a boy, not then more than ten years old, I rose at seven o'clock, sometimes earlier, and with my father and brothers trudged through cold, empty streets to our synagogue in South Terrace. There, under the watchful eyes of so many old campaigners, we learned by rote the right prayer, at the right hour, and in the right place, and then home to a piping-hot breakfast prepared by our mother, for we were not allowed to quench the thirst or satisfy our appetites until the first prayer of the day was pronounced by our father:

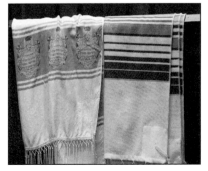

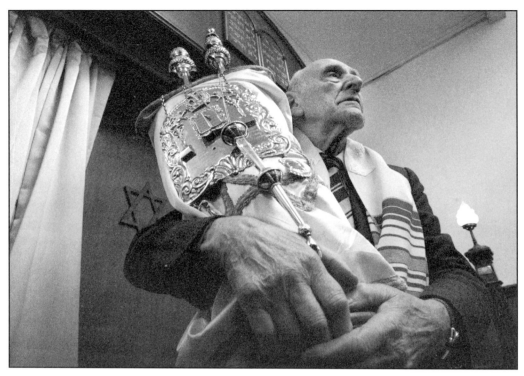

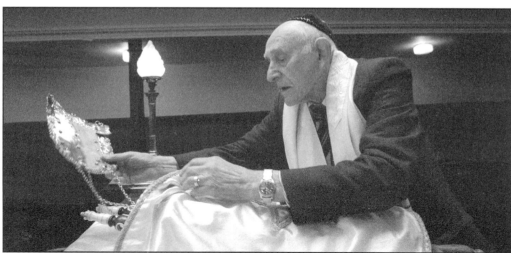

These pictures were taken at the synagogue in South Terrace Cork city

Blessed are thou, O Lord our God, King of the Universe,
Who bringeth forth bread from the earth.

But this is not for all, there is a beginning and an end. There is a time in the evening when sleep overtakes us and we retire to rest. So, during my lifetime, and over my bed, hangs a Hebrew prayer resplendent in the immaculate engravings of the late Elizabeth Friedlander who sleeps her sleep among the members of my family thus:

Cause us, O Lord, to lie down in peace,
And raise us up, O our King, into life.
Spread o'er us the tabernacle of thy peace;
Direct us aright through thine own good counsel;
Save us for thy name's sake; be thou a shield about us;
Remove from us every enemy, pestilence, sword, famine and sorrow;
Remove also adversary from before us and behind us;
O shelter us beneath the shadow of thy wings;
For thou, O God, art our guardian and our deliverer;
Yea, thou, O God, art a gracious and merciful King;
And guard our going out of our coming in
Unto life and unto peace from this time forth and forever more;
Yea, spread over us the tabernacle of thy peace.
Blessed art thou, O God, who spreadest the tabernacle of peace over us
And over all thy people Israel, and over Jerusalem.

And with that we say "Good night".'

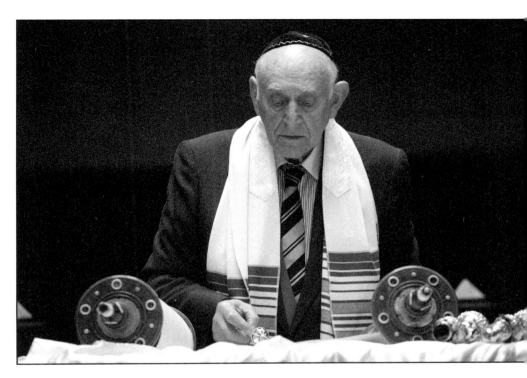

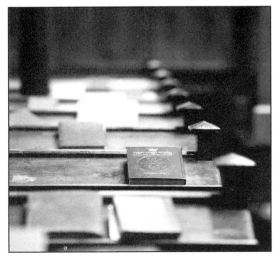

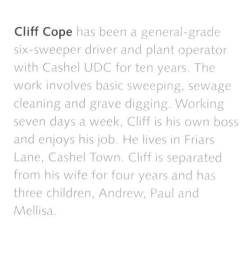
Cliff Cope has been a general-grade six-sweeper driver and plant operator with Cashel UDC for ten years. The work involves basic sweeping, sewage cleaning and grave digging. Working seven days a week, Cliff is his own boss and enjoys his job. He lives in Friars Lane, Cashel Town. Cliff is separated from his wife for four years and has three children, Andrew, Paul and Mellisa.

'Paul, my second son, has cerebral palsy. He is just ten years old, and it makes you realise how lucky you are in life. When I see him he has such a big smile on his face, I wonder what I am so miserable for. He has more on his shoulders than we'll ever know.

Paul goes to a school for children with special needs. At the moment he is learning to use a computer with his teacher, Aileen. Paul has no movement in his hands. He cannot walk and has no control. With a special button to the side of his head, linked from his chair to a computer screen, he can ask for the basic things – especially his favourite "chocky biccies".

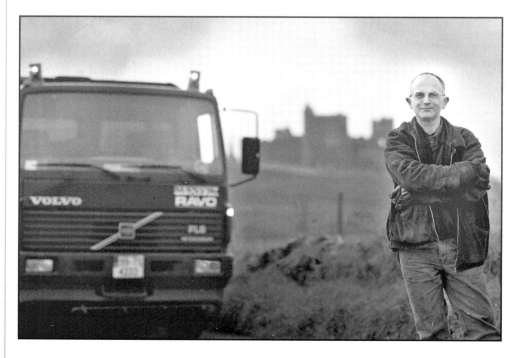

Cliff Cope on his daily route, with the Rock of Cashel in the distance

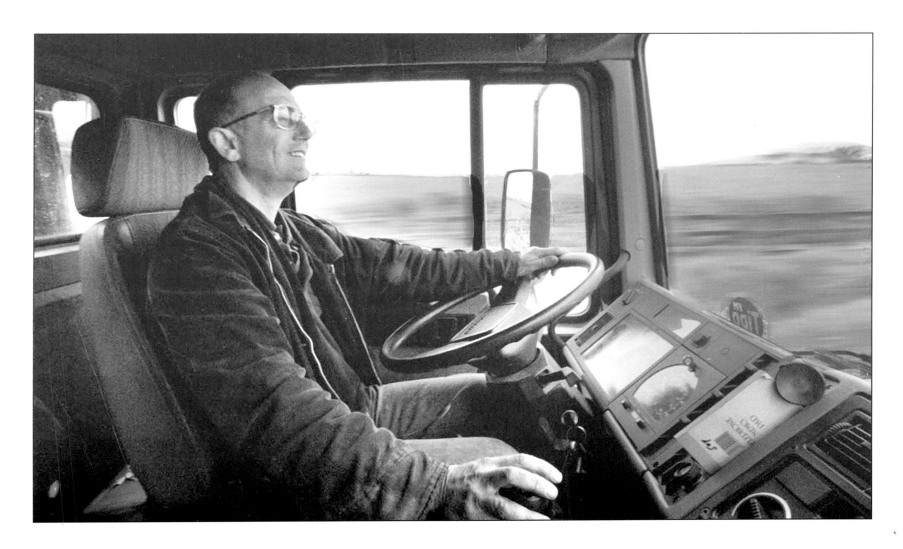

Paul brings tremendous joy to my life. When I take him into town on Saturdays, everybody knows him...he's incredible, he always remembers people's faces and never forgets anybody...the smile on his face really tells it all. I watch his eyes light up, which puts me to shame, because he has so many problems. He never asks for anything. He is so happy and contented, so special...that's my fellah.'

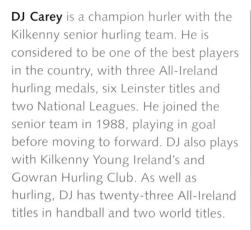

DJ Carey is a champion hurler with the Kilkenny senior hurling team. He is considered to be one of the best players in the country, with three All-Ireland hurling medals, six Leinster titles and two National Leagues. He joined the senior team in 1988, playing in goal before moving to forward. DJ also plays with Kilkenny Young Ireland's and Gowran Hurling Club. As well as hurling, DJ has twenty-three All-Ireland titles in handball and two world titles.

He is Director of DJ Carey Enterprises, who sell hygiene and detergent products all over the country. He is married to Christine and they have two children, Seán and Michael. DJ is a native of Gowran, County Kilkenny, and is a member of Callan Golf Club and Mount Juliet.

'Being from Kilkenny makes me very proud. Hurling is such an important sport to the Kilkenny people. I am delighted with my career and how it's gone so far. The training for the championship is always very intense and involves total dedication. I am very committed and dedicated to the game. I don't drink or smoke. Teamwork is very important. I have played on a team since I was eight years old and I know what it takes. The vigorous training four and five nights a week is tough but very rewarding. As amateurs we play nine months of the year. When you have a talent, especially a sporting talent, be thankful for your gift, and always use it to the best of your ability.'

*DJ Carey with his two year old son Seán
already mastering the game of hurling*

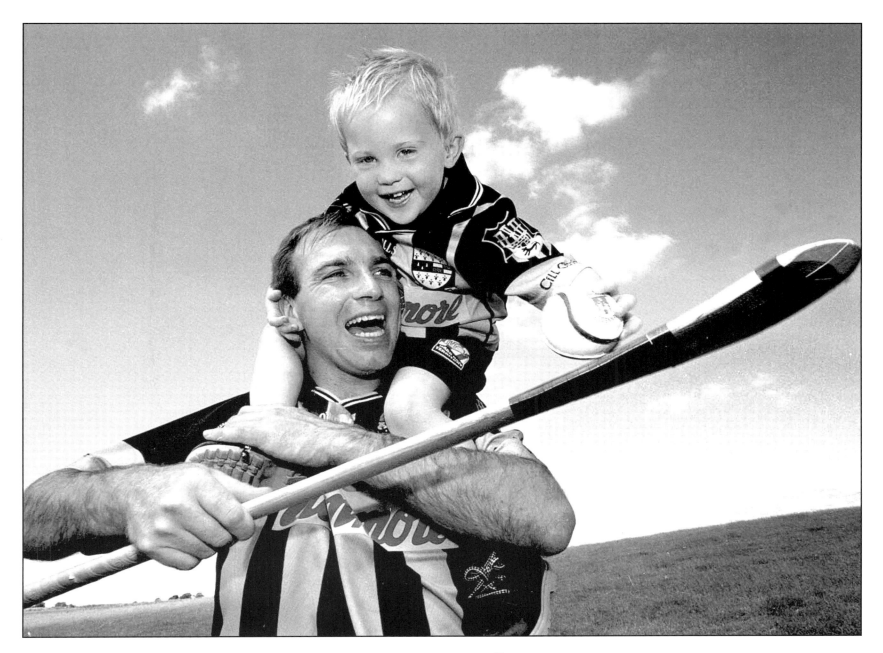

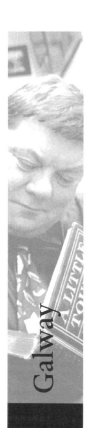

Galway

Dessie Kenny

Dessie Kenny is a bookseller and is Director of Kenny's Bookshop on High Street in Galway City. The family-run bookshop has been an institution in Ireland for 50 years, specialising in books of Irish interest and selling books world-wide. Kenny's was one of the first bookshops in the world to have a web-site, and Dessie takes great pride in responding to his customers each morning by e-mail. A native of Galway City, he is married to Anne Gilmartin and they have four children, Deirdre, Dessie, Aisling and Eimear. Dessie studied in UCG and undertook a masters in Paris. He enjoys all books, good stories, and good conversation. His mother Maureen Kenny still works in the family shop.

'There are three things that lift my soul.
The melody of children – especially if in French chatter,
A long country road, crooked and empty, and the sun behind me.'

Men's curiosity searches past and future
And clings to that dimension. But to apprehend
The point of interaction of the timeless
With time, is an occupation for the saint –
No occupation either, but something given
And taken, in a lifetime's death in love,
Ardour and selflessness and self-surrender.
For most of us, there is only the unattended
Moment, the moment in and out of time,
The distraction fit, lost in a shaft of sunlight
The wild thyme unseen, or the winter lightning
Or the waterfall, or music heard so deeply
That it is not heard at all, but you are the music
While the music lasts.

from 'The Dry Salvages' by T. S. Eliot (1888–1965)

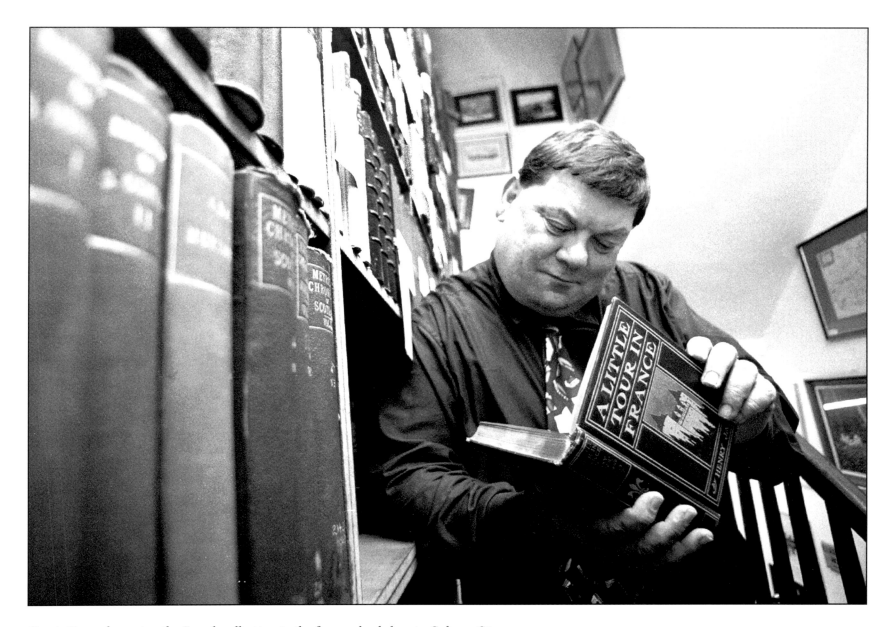

Dessie Kenny browsing the French collection in the famous bookshop in Galway City

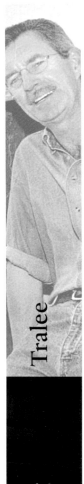

Dick Spring is a TD for North Kerry. He became a member of Dáil Éireann in 1981 and was leader of the Labour Party for fifteen years. As well as being Tánaiste in three Governments, he held ministries in the Departments of Justice, Environment, and Foreign Affairs. Dick is a graduate of Trinity College, Dublin, and Kings Inn, and practised law prior to becoming a TD.

He holds a number of non-executive directorships and acts as international counsel for the Boston- and Washington-based law firm, Mintz Levin Cohn Ferris Glovsky and Popeo. He is married to Kristi and they have three children, Aaron, Laura and Adam. He enjoys golfing and reading.

'Being born in Strand Road, Tralee, in 1950, makes me a very proud Kerryman. Kerry is a great place to live and work and raise a family. It is important to make a contribution to our society and to leave things a little better than how we found them.'

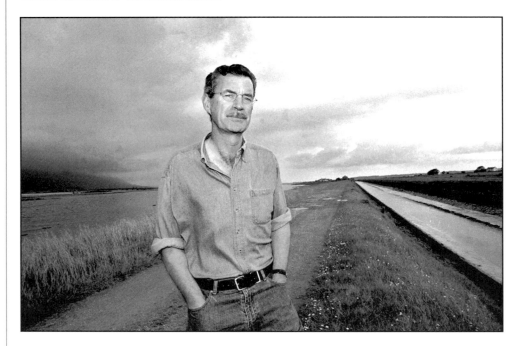

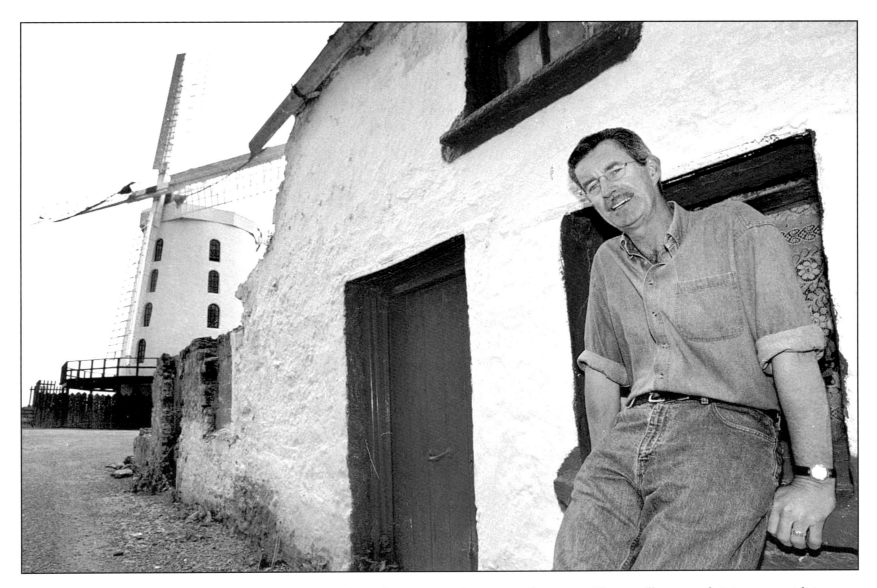

Dick Spring is pictured in Blennerville village, just outside Tralee town. In the nineteenth century, Blennerville was a thriving port with its own windmill. It was from here that the famous Jennie Johnston set sail for America during the famine years in Ireland. Fortunately, the ship never lost a passenger in all its treacherous Atlantic crossings.

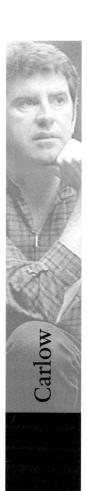

Liam Lawton is an established Irish composer specialising in liturgical and sacred music. Based in Carlow, he is director of music in the Diocese of Kildare and Leighlin, and conducts music workshops throughout the world. Liam is on the board of the Irish Church Music Association and the Irish Church Commission for Sacred Music. He publishes with GIA (USA) and Veritas (Dublin). Originally from Edenderry, County Offaly, his family includes parents Tom and May, brothers Tom (his twin), Gabriel and John, and sister Marie. He has recorded six albums to date, including *The Shepherd Boy*, *The Cloud's Veil*, *Light the Fire*, *Sacred Stone*, *Molaise* and *Ancient ways, Future days*. Liam edited a new national collection of hymns called *In Caelo* in 1999. He has worked with The Vard Sisters, Aoife Ní Fhearraigh and the chamber choir Lumina, who have recently recorded 'Heaven's door' for a new millennium collection of Irish composers. Liam enjoys reading, travel and music. He is currently studying at the Irish World Music Centre at the University of Limerick.

'In my composing, I have always found myself being drawn back to the richness of our Celtic heritage. It has much to teach us today, in its lack of distinction between religion and daily life, between the spiritual and the material realms. It was the faith that permeated every aspect of existence, and it brought with it a respect for humankind and the natural surroundings – all crafted by the same master-craftsman. Many of the beautiful prayers and poems from the past come down to us by word of mouth and are filled with an emotional intensity that can still inspire us today.'

The Mystery

I am the wind which breathes upon the sea,
I am the wave of the ocean,
I am the murmur of the billows,
I am the ox of the seven combats.
I am the vulture on the rocks,
I am the beam of the sun,
I am the fairest of plants,
I am the wild boar in valour,
I am the salmon in the water,
I am the lake in the plain,
I am the word of science,
I am the point of the lance of battle,
I am the God who created in the head of fire.
Who is it who throws light into the meeting on the mountain?
Who announces the ages of the moon?
Who teaches the place where crouches the sun?
(If not I)

Amergin (sixth-century poet), translated by Douglas Hyde (1860–1949)

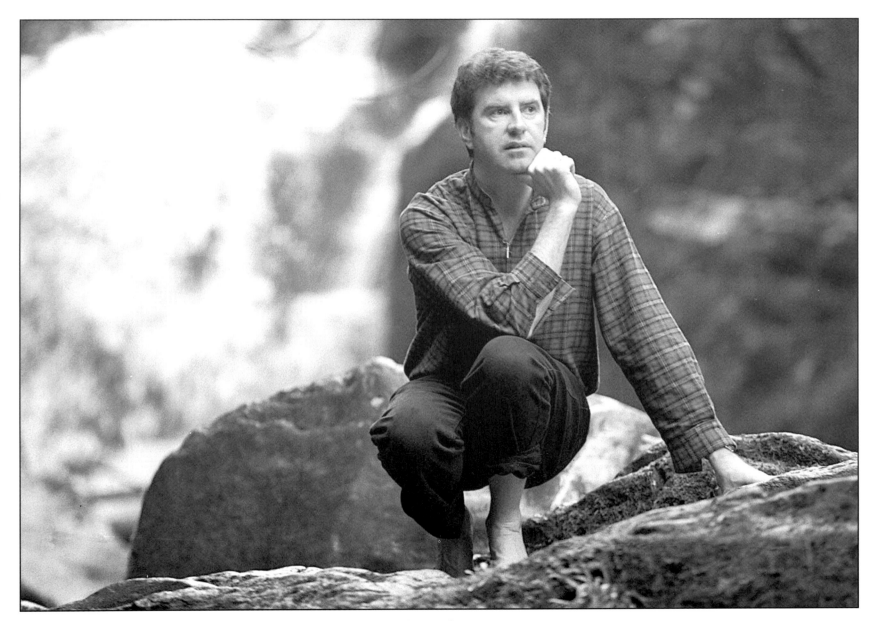

Irish composer Liam Lawton, in tune with nature and the ancient Celtic traditions

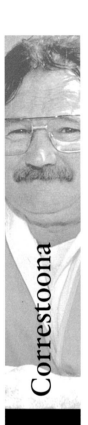

Correstoona

Pat Colleran

Pat Colleran is the gatekeeper at Correstoona Cross, County Roscommon, manning the gates eight times a day. He is a native of Adragoole, Castlerea, where his father and mother, Peter and Kathleen, manned the gates for sixty years. Pat has worked at the cross for six years, after returning from England where he worked for a scaffolding company. He is married to Brigid and has four children, Peter, Helen, Susan and Sharon, and twelve grandchildren. He is a collector of antique clocks, which he repairs and restores to their former glory. He also enjoys farming and fishing, and breeds peacocks.

'I remember as a young child watching my Uncle Paddy repairing clocks. He also worked on the permanent way and I stayed with him on my holidays. I was fascinated as to how the pendulum could be three feet in length and weigh fourteen pounds. I wondered how it could keep swinging; it always amazes me. I found a clock, a Joseph Nibbs dated 1690, and restored it. Since then, I have collected and restored hundreds of clocks.

In my job you are always watching the time; you look at a clock a thousand times a day. Time is very important to us all, not only in its significance at the gates, but time itself, when you remember your parents and times past. In the future, should this cross ever be automated, time will still be important. I can't do without a watch, even it is only making silage or calving. You can't do without time...'

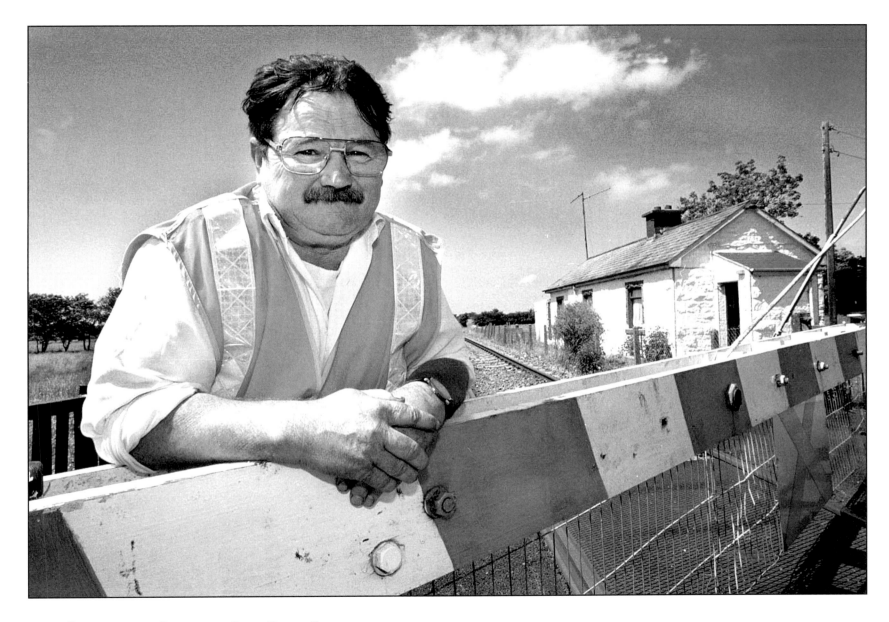

Pat Colleran manning Correstoona Cross, County Roscommon

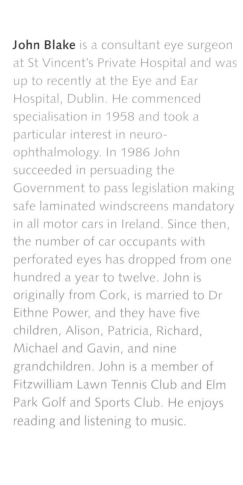

Dublin

John Blake

John Blake is a consultant eye surgeon at St Vincent's Private Hospital and was up to recently at the Eye and Ear Hospital, Dublin. He commenced specialisation in 1958 and took a particular interest in neuro-ophthalmology. In 1986 John succeeded in persuading the Government to pass legislation making safe laminated windscreens mandatory in all motor cars in Ireland. Since then, the number of car occupants with perforated eyes has dropped from one hundred a year to twelve. John is originally from Cork, is married to Dr Eithne Power, and they have five children, Alison, Patricia, Richard, Michael and Gavin, and nine grandchildren. John is a member of Fitzwilliam Lawn Tennis Club and Elm Park Golf and Sports Club. He enjoys reading and listening to music.

'"When smiling, when smiling, the whole world smiles with you.
When laughing, when laughing, the sun comes shining through".

Or more formally: The mind is a place of its own and can make a heaven of hell and hell of heaven.'

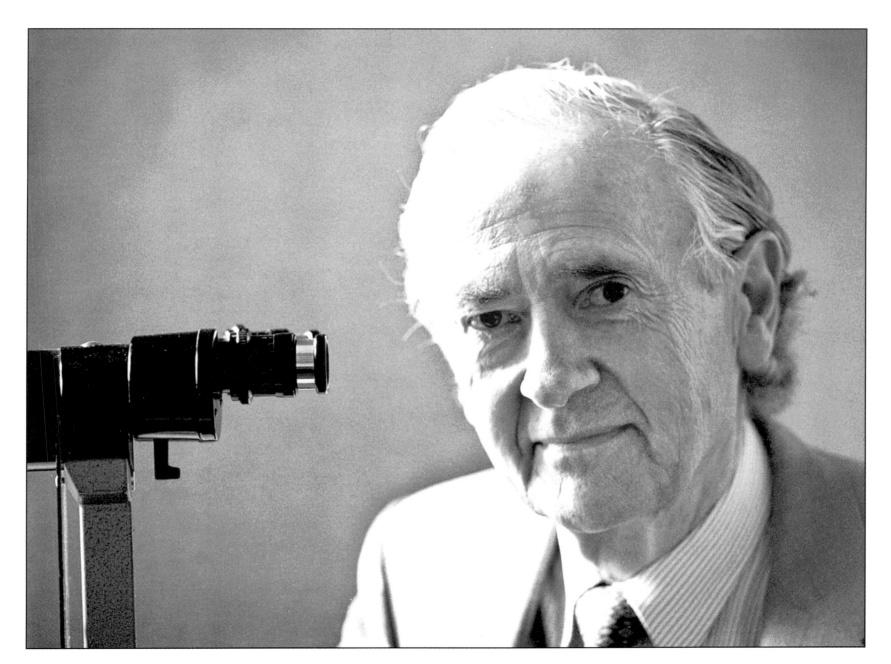

Tom Moore is manager of the ancient monastic site at Clonmacnoise, County Offaly, a historic site that now attracts 140,000 visitors a year. A native of Clonmacnoise, Tom began working there in 1973 as a tour guide. He is married to Rosemary Higgins and is a farmer also. Tom has a great interest in heritage and conservation and when abroad loves to compare the different heritage and cultures. He enjoys all sport and has played with Shannonbridge GAA Club and Moore United Soccer Club.

'When St Ciarán founded Clonmacnoise in AD 548, his intention was to form a monastery that would act as a place of prayer and gathering for all Christians. Unfortunately, over the years, and right up to the last century, there was a huge divide between those communities. Thankfully, however, in this millennium, the site is being shared by all denominations and the impetus and sentiment of Clonmacnoise as a place of welcome, and a space to reflect on times past, has returned.'

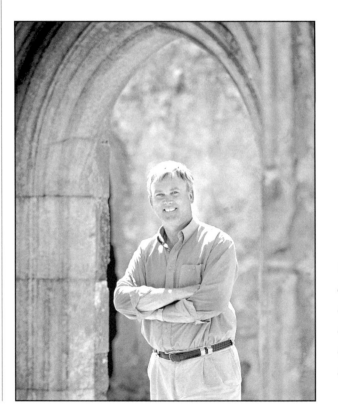

Clonmacnoise is one of the country's most celebrated ecclesiastical sites. It has a cathedral, eight ruined churches, three high crosses and two round towers.

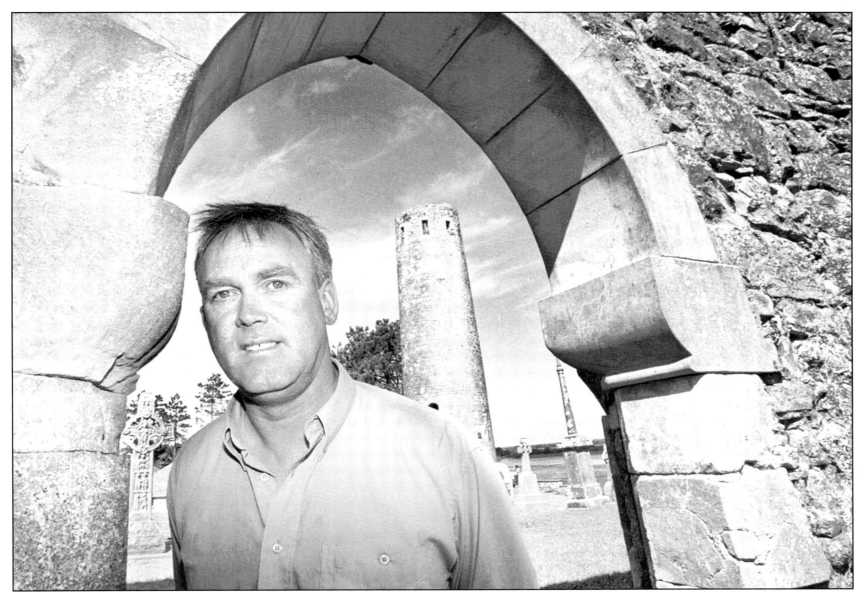

Tom Moore stands in front of the renowned 'Cross of the Scriptures' or 'King Flann's Cross', which depicts scenes from the Last Judgement and Crucifixion of Christ.

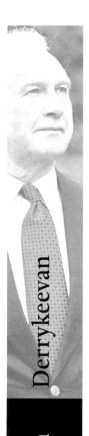

Derrykeevan

Samuel G. Benson

Samuel George Benson has lived all his life on a family farm in the townland of Derrykeevan, three miles from Portadown and close to Lough Neagh. He is Worshipful Master of the local lodge (LOL 352) and has served on the select vestry of the parish church for many years. Samuel is married to Mary and they have three children, David, who now takes responsibility for the dairy herd, Catherine, and George.

'I have been a member of the Orange Institution since the age of eighteen and I hold the office of Worshipful Master of the local lodge. As an Orangeman, I believe in civil and religious liberty for all and am saddened that in this land there are so many people who are unwilling to show any tolerance for any tradition other than their own. The Orange Lodge encourages its members to be strong in their Protestant faith. One of the Bible readings used in the initiation ceremony of an Orangeman is from Ephesians (6:10-13):

Be strong in the Lord, and in the power of his might. Put on the whole armour of God, that ye may be able to stand against the wiles of the devil. For we wrestle not against flesh and blood, but against principalities, against rulers of the darkness of this world, against spiritual wickedness in high places. Wherefore take unto you the whole armour of God, that ye may be able to stand in the evil way.

I feel these words are good advice for anyone, especially in today's world when the Christian faith and Christian family values are being eroded on every side.'

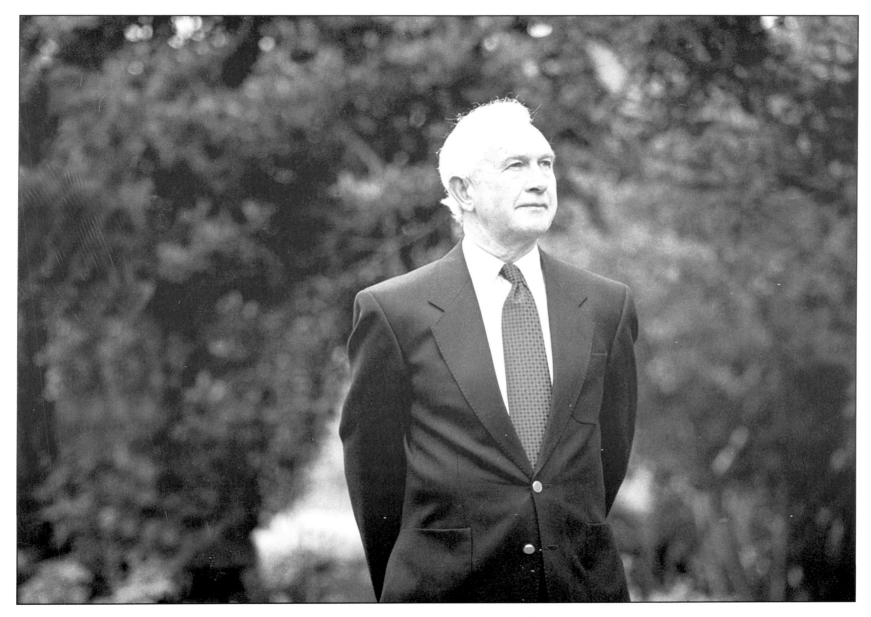

Samuel Benson has been a member of the Local Orange Lodge since he was eighteen years old

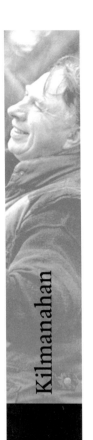

Kilmanahan

Tom White

Tom White has been farm manager at Showerings Orchards, Clonmel, for the past twenty-three years. His work involves planting, pruning, maintaining and harvesting the crop. Showerings press twenty thousand tons of apples annually, producing Bulmer's Cider, Cidona, Ritz and Stag. Tom is a native of Kilmanahan, County Waterford. He is married to Marie White and they have three children, David, TJ and Olivia. He is also a part-time farmer, and enjoys all GAA sport and country and western music.

Lo! Sweeten'd with the summer light,
The full-juiced apple, waxing over-
mellow,
Drops in a silent autumn night.
All its allotted length of days
The flower ripens in its place,
Ripens and fades, and falls, and hath no
toil,
Fast-rooted in the fruitful soil.

from 'The Lotus-Eaters'
by Alfred Lord Tennyson (1809–92)

I gazed – and gazed – but little thought
What wealth the show to me had
brought.

from 'The Daffodils'
by William Wordsworth (1770–1850)

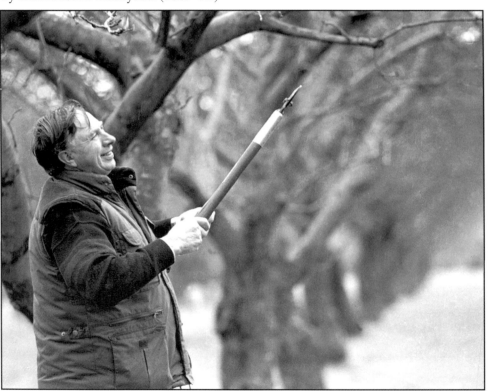

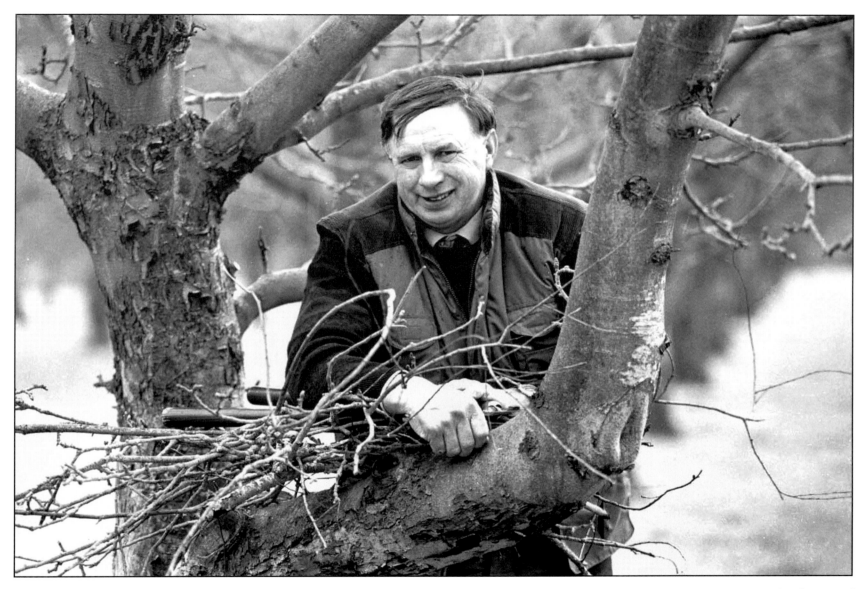

'These extracts reflect the view of the work I carry out. I love my job. I have a great love for the land and surroundings. Springtime is a lovely time of the year – watching the crop develop and blossom right through to harvest time…it's as close to nature as you'll ever get.'

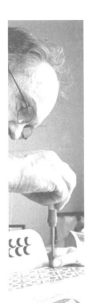

Martin Connolly is an accordion maker based in Ennis, County Clare. Making the renowned Kincora Accordion, he set up his business at home four years ago. Prior to that he repaired and tuned instruments. An accomplished musician himself, Martin is a native of Killaloe, County Clare. His wife Maureen Glynn, also a well-known musician, died just over a year ago. She played fiddle and piano. Martin has two children, Damien and Karl, who play piano and accordion. Martin loves his music, his faithful dog Ted, and is also a keen soccer supporter.

'Make the most out of life, we're here for a good time, not a long time. My wife passed away a short time ago. Looking back on everything, I know now that I could have enjoyed life a lot more. She was only forty-six years old and died after a short illness. Now I'm very thankful for every morning I wake up to. When I was going through the early grieving stage, I wanted to be with Maureen as well. Now, as every day passes, I realise I have to enjoy life and get on with living. That's my philosophy: We're here for a good time, not a long time...'

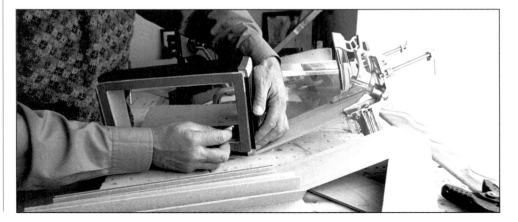

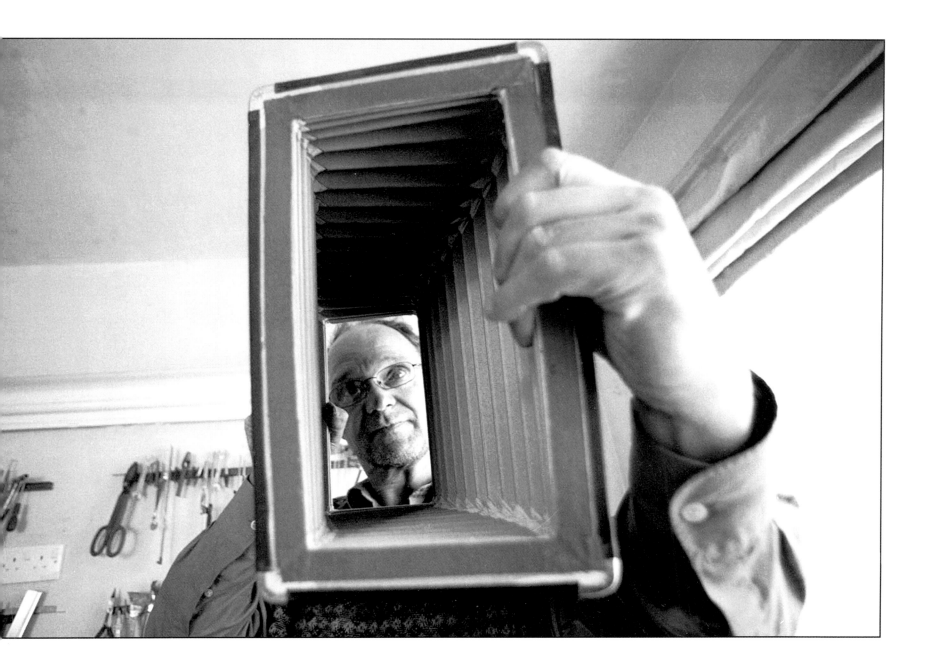

My Father played the melodion
Outside at our gate;
There were stars in the morning east
And they danced to his music.

Across the wild bogs his melodion called
To Lennons and Callans.
As I pulled on my trousers in a hurry
I knew some strange thing had happened.

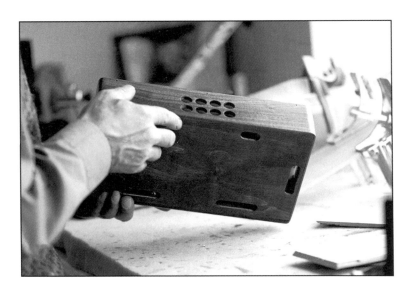

Outside in the cow-house my mother
Made the music of milking;
The light of her stable-lamp was a star
And the frost of Bethlehem made it twinkle.

A water-hen screeched in the bog,
Mass-going feet
Crunched the wafer-ice on the pot-holes,
Somebody wistfully twisted the bellows wheel.

....

An old man passing said:
'Can't he make it talk' –
The melodion. I hid in the doorway
And tightened the belt of my box-pleated coat.

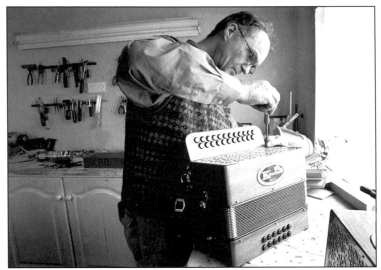

....

from 'A Christmas Childhood'
by Patrick Kavanagh (1904–67)

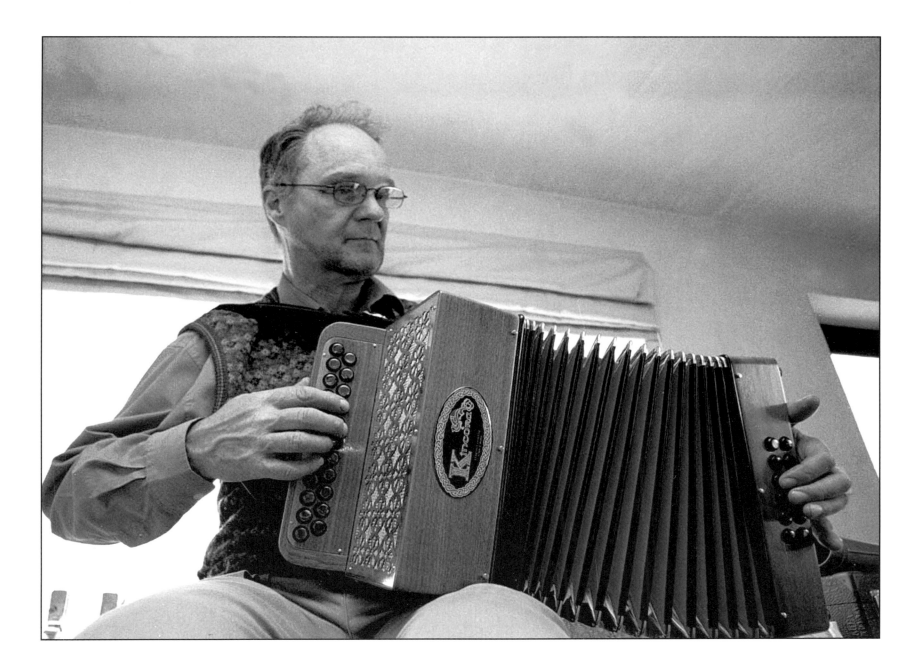

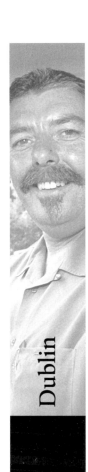

Matt Gannon is a taxi owner who has worked in Dublin City for the past eleven years. Prior to that he was a milkman in Castleknock. As a taxi driver he works long hours, covering day and night shifts. A native of City Quay, Finglas, Matt is married to Lillian Fitzgibbon and they have three children, Rowena, Grace and Danielle. He enjoys gardening, walking in the Botanic Gardens, music and socialising.

'When I started my career as a taxi-driver, I was innocent of people. I meet people of all walks of life, both famous and infamous; that's the beauty of my job. The night work can be really tough. Dublin has changed so much in the last five years, everyone has much more money to spend. As a driver I am all things to all people...a priest, counsellor, tour-guide, doctor and consoler of broken hearts! Very often, people tell you things about themselves that they couldn't tell anybody else. I have developed a great sense of the customer. You tend to develop that skill in this job.'

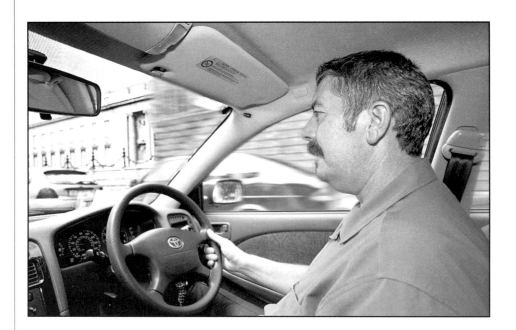

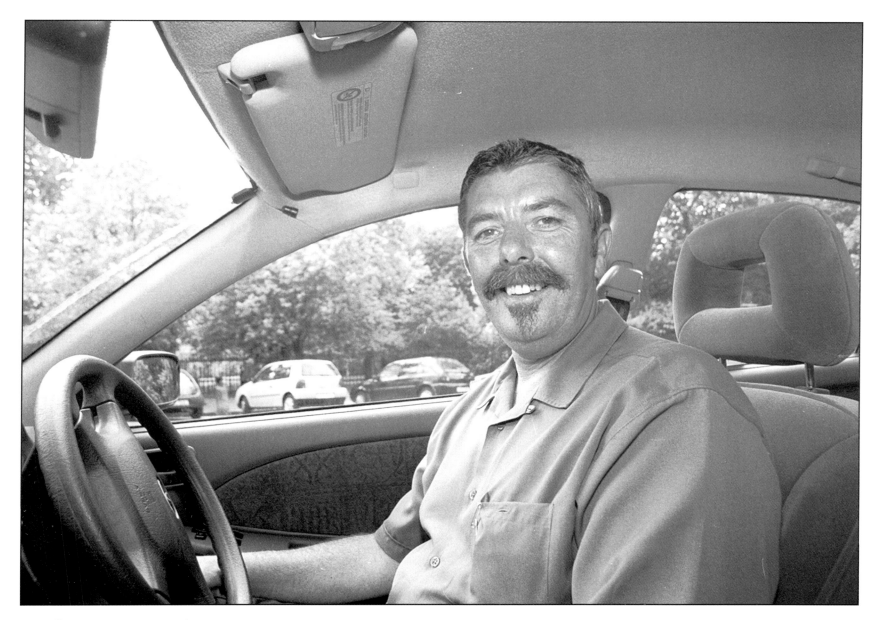

Matt Gannon at your service!

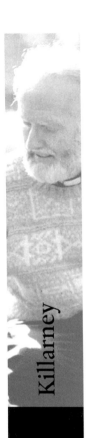

Killarney

Brian Lougheed

Brian Lougheed is Church of Ireland rector of Killarney and Aghadoe Union, carrying out pastoral duties with a continual influx of tourists from different congregations. He was made a Canon of St Patrick's National Cathedral in 1990. A native of Kinnitty and Clara, County Offaly, he is a fourth generation clergyman. He studied in Sligo Grammar High and Trinity College, Dublin. Prior to his appointment in Killarney in 1990, he carried out pastoral duties in Dublin and Rathmolyan. Brian is a Trustee of Muckross House, Chairman of Muckross Church Adventure Centre, and a Knight of Innisfallen. His wife Norma died in 1985 and he has three children, Heather, Andrew and Siobhán, and a faithful four-legged friend, Cassidy. Brian enjoys reading thrillers and travel books, listening to classical music, travel, photography and any good party!

'I'm not good at structured prayer. I find that when praying about a situation, you have to be active in the problems you are praying about. For me, every baptized Christian is part of Christ's body on earth and must get on with what he did, and not just praying. This prayer is a reminder that we have to be involved in doing things. Jesus went about doing good; we suffer from too many people claiming his name who are just going about.'

St Theresa's Prayer

Christ has no body on earth, but yours
No hands, but yours
No feet, but yours
Yours are the eyes
Through which is to look out
Christ's compassion to the world
Yours are the feet with which he walks to do good
Yours are the hands with which he is
To bless men now.

This is when everything is going wrong and I feel like throwing the whole thing out:

Turn thy face from my sins;
and put out of my best deed,
make me a clean heart
and renew a right spirit within me.

from Psalm 51

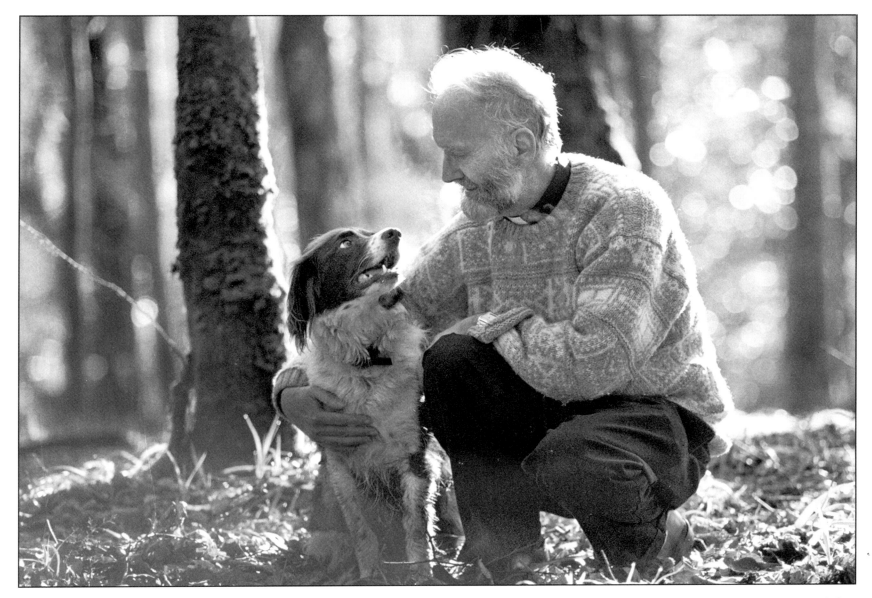

'In certain company, my prayer is: God grant me the company of those who are seeking the truth, but preserve me from those who are convinced they have found it.'

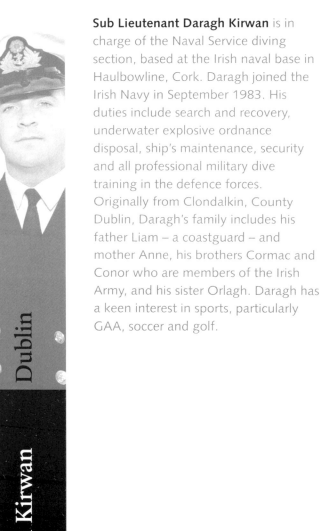

Sub Lieutenant Daragh Kirwan is in charge of the Naval Service diving section, based at the Irish naval base in Haulbowline, Cork. Daragh joined the Irish Navy in September 1983. His duties include search and recovery, underwater explosive ordnance disposal, ship's maintenance, security and all professional military dive training in the defence forces. Originally from Clondalkin, County Dublin, Daragh's family includes his father Liam – a coastguard – and mother Anne, his brothers Cormac and Conor who are members of the Irish Army, and his sister Orlagh. Daragh has a keen interest in sports, particularly GAA, soccer and golf.

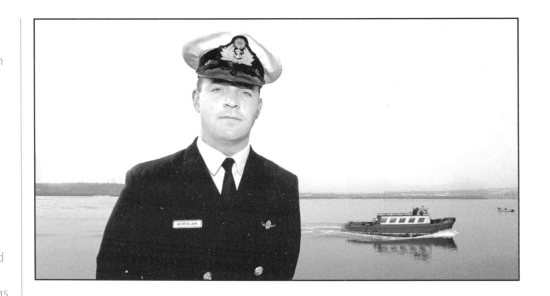

Roll on, thou deep and dark blue ocean-roll!
Ten thousand fleets sweep over thee in vain;
Man marks the earth with ruin – his control
Stops with the shore.

from 'Childe Harold's Pilgrimage' by Lord Byron (1788–1824)

Sub Lieutenant Daragh Kirwan carries out his daily duties at the naval base in Haulbowline, Cork

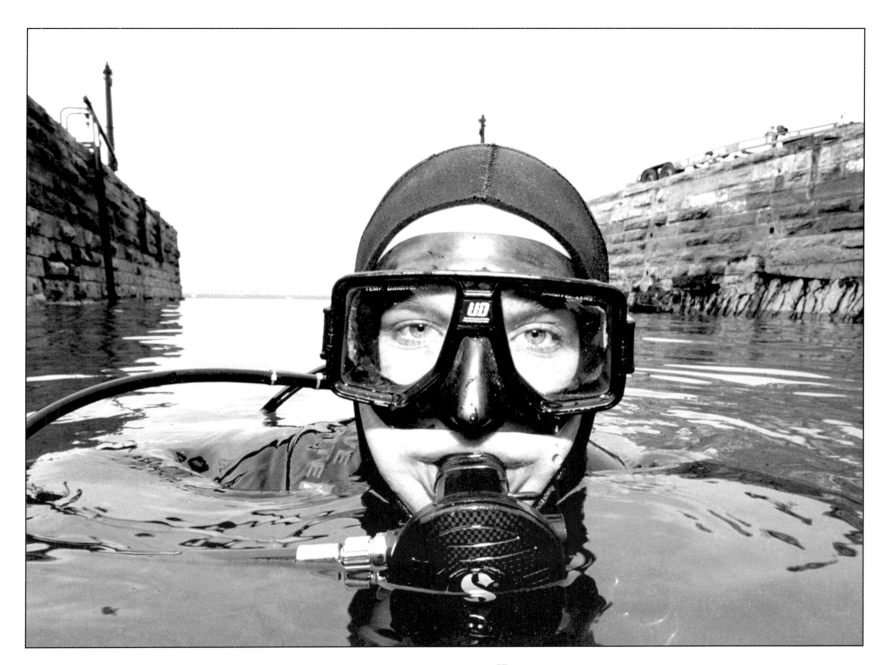

Dublin

David Quinn

David Quinn is editor of *The Irish Catholic* newspaper, and a columnist with *The Sunday Times*. He is a frequent contributor to both radio and television. Prior to his appointment as editor he was a journalist with *The Sunday Business Post,* and before that he worked in an investment company in Australia where he met his wife Rachael. They have one son Luc who is two years old. David is originally from Clontarf, County Dublin, and has three sisters, Anne, Oonagh and Kathyrn. He has a BSc in Business Studies from Dublin City University and in his free time he enjoys playing tennis

If

If you can keep your head when all about you
Are losing theirs and blaming it on you;
If you can trust yourself when all men doubt you,
But make allowance for their doubting too;
If you can wait and not be tired by waiting,
Or, being lied about, don't deal in lies,
Or, being hated, don't give way to hating,
And yet don't look too good, nor talk too wise;

If you can dream – and not make dreams your master;
If you can think – and not make thoughts your aim;
If you can meet with triumph and disaster
And treat those two impostors just the same;
If you can bear to hear the truth you've spoken
Twisted by knaves to make a trap for fools,
Or watch the things you gave your life to broken,
And stoop and build 'em up with wornout tools;

If you can make one heap of all your winnings
And risk it on one turn of pitch-and-toss,
And lose, and start again at your beginnings
And never breathe a word about your loss;
If you can force your heart and nerve and sinew
To serve your turn long after they are gone,
And so hold on when there is nothing in you
Except the Will which says to them: "Hold on";

If you can talk with crowds and keep your virtue,
Or walk with kings – nor lose the common touch;
If neither foes nor loving friends can hurt you;
If all men count with you, but none too much;
If you can fill the unforgiving minute
With sixty seconds' worth of distance run –
Yours is the Earth and everything that's in it,
And – which is more – you'll be a Man my son!

Rudyard Kipling (1865–1936)

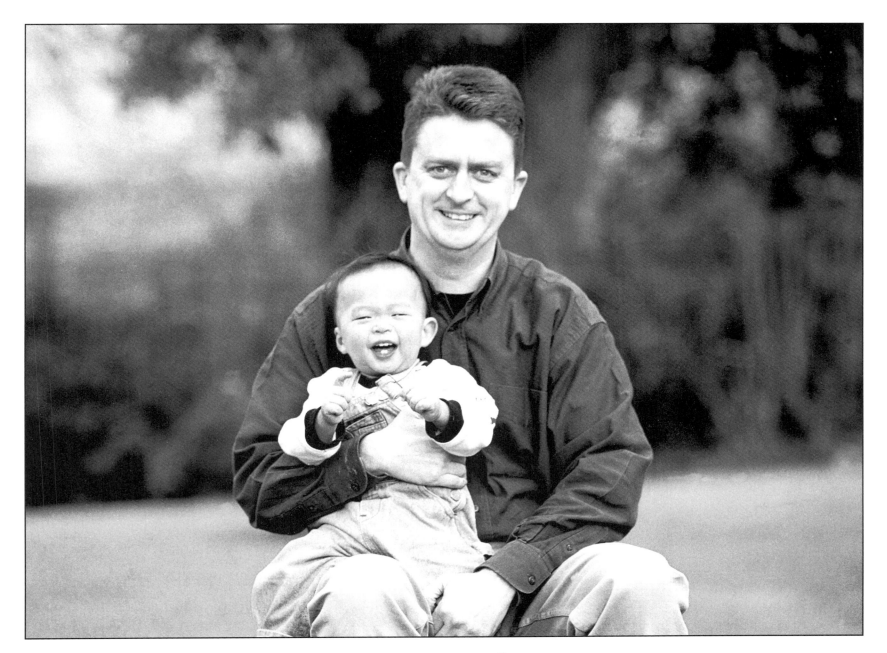

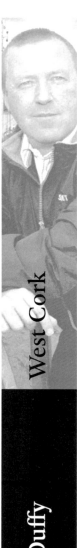

West Cork

Niall Duffy

Niall Duffy is sales manager of a European electronic fish-auction company based in Belgium. He is introducing the internet to fishermen, who are one of the last bastions of old-style auctioning. Niall is originally from Chapelizod, County Dublin, and now lives in west Cork with his partner Marie Noelle and their son Louis. Niall is a former fisherman and marine photographer and enjoys photography, fishing and reading.

Sea Fever

I must go down to the seas again, to the lonely sea and the sky,
And all I ask is a tall ship and a star to steer her by,
And the wheel's kick and the wind's song and the white sail's shaking,
And a gray mist on the sea's face, and a gray dawn breaking.

I must go down to the seas again, for the call of the running tide
Is a wild call and a clear call that may not be denied;
And all I ask is a windy day with the white clouds flying,
And the flung spray and the blown spume, and the sea-gulls crying.

I must go down to the seas again, to the vagrant gypsy life,
To the gull's way and the whale's way, where the wind's like a whetted knife;
And all I ask is a merry yarn from a laughing fellow-rover,
And quiet sleep and a sweet dream when the long trick's over.

John Masefield (1878–1967)

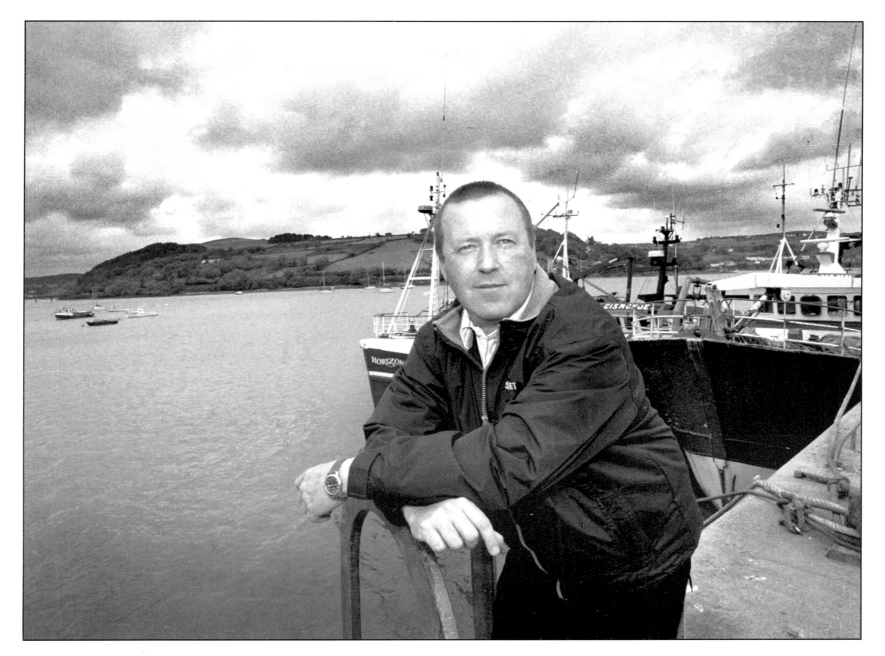

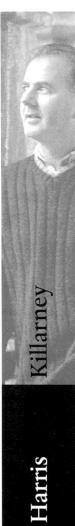

Killarney

Michael Harris

Michael Harris has been guardian at the Franciscan friary in Killarney since 1996. Prior to this, he was guardian at the friary in Cork City. Much of his work is in pastoral care. He is a native of Clonmel, County Tipperary, and studied in University College, Galway, and in Rome. Michael is a trustee of Muckross House, Killarney, is a chaplin to Killarney Community College, and is on the development committee of the new Killarney Youth Centre at the friary. He has seven sisters and five brothers, Kate, Rose, Margaret, Helen, Rita, Caroline, Ann-marie, Robert, Eddie, Joe, Anthony and John, and his mother Rose still resides in Clonmel. He enjoys walking, cycling, music and watching a good hurling game.

'Sometimes I meet people in the course of my ministry who say, "What I need right now is a miracle!", or they might ask, "Are there such things today as miracles?", and I say "Yes, miracles are happening every day around us and a lot of the time we are not able to see them."

Jean Vanier, founder of the world-wide L'Arche Communities, is a man I very much admire, because of the kind of person he is and what he believes in. One of his strong beliefs is in "the everyday miracle". In his writings he gives many examples of miracles that he has experienced in his life and ministry. He says that when people who have a mental disability are locked away, they wither. Their hearts and spirits are damaged. He has witnessed the "miracle of change". Vanier tells the story of Vivienne, who came to his community some years back. She was blind and autistic. She had never experienced a permanent relationship. At the start she couldn't cope. She screamed and screamed, and even bit at the helpers. Then, after some time and encouragement, she discovered that she was loved. She began to feel secure. She had a new spirit…a new heart. Vivienne heard the three most important words that we all need to hear and experience: I love you.

People change if they can get rid of guilt, shame and fears. They change when they are given hope. They change when someone believes in them and gives them responsibility. They change when someone takes an interest in them. Above all, people change when they are loved. That is the miracle of human change. It is indeed a real miracle. Which of us can say we don't need change? To live is to change; to be perfect is to have changed often.'

Lord, Grant me the serenity
To accept the things I cannot change,
The courage to change the things I can,
And the wisdom to know the difference.

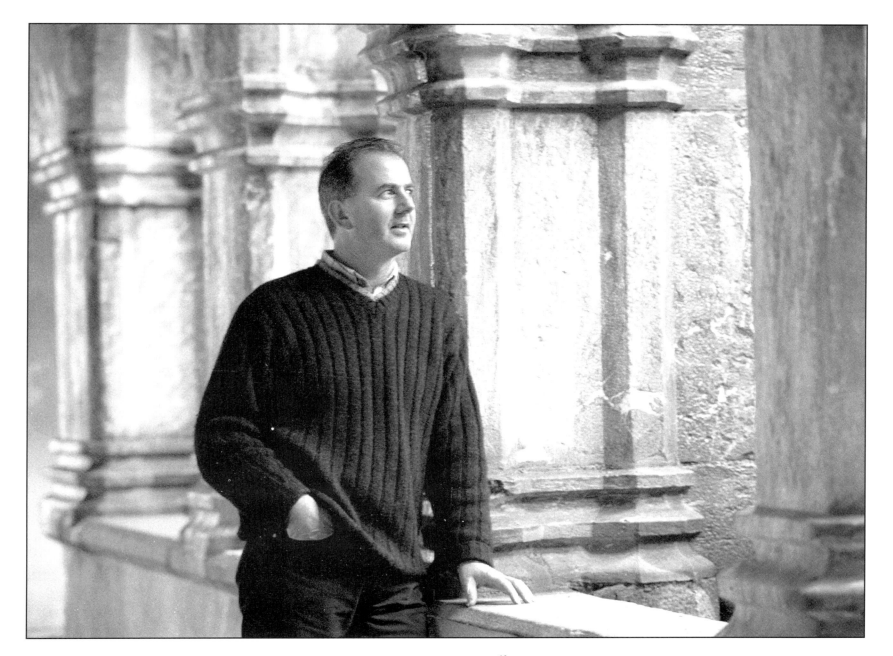

Patrick Casey is a photographer based in north Cork. He works for many newspapers and publications, most notably *The Corkman*. He also works with IRD Duhallow and Millstreet International Horse Show. He is a native of Kanturk, County Cork, but now lives in Mallow. Patrick has two brothers, Tony and Giles, and two sisters, Synthia and Mary. His mother, Nilla Casey, lives in the family home in Kanturk. Patrick enjoys music, cinema and drama.

Kanturk

Patrick Casey

'Choose life at whatever risk. In keeping your head under the cover, nothing will ever happen to you…good or bad…so take the plunge!'

Patrick Casey at the entrance to Kanturk Castle; the old court castle was begun in 1609 by MacDonagh MacCarthy, Lord of Dunhallow, and was never completed.

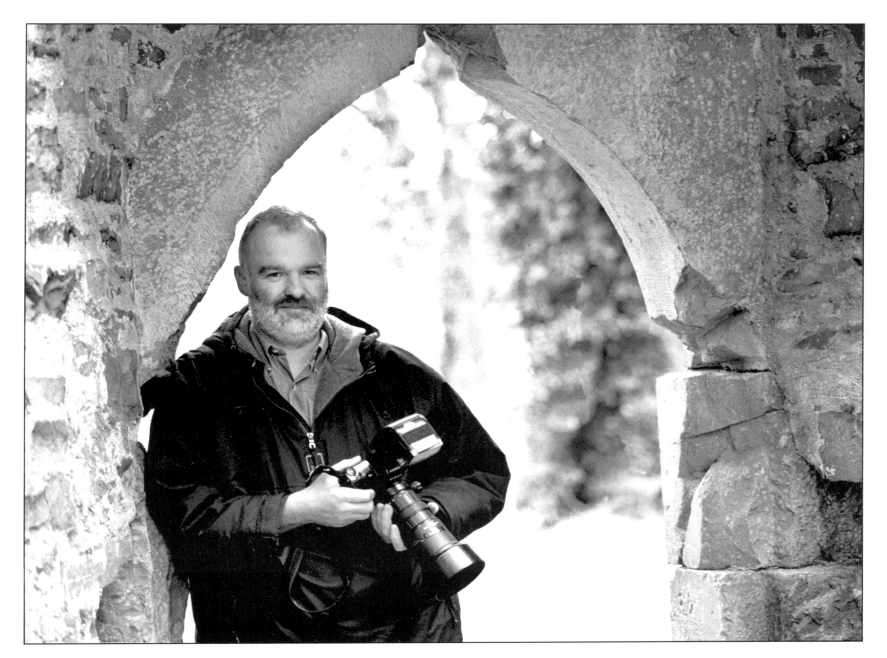

Chick (Michael) Gillen has been a barber in Dominic Street, Galway city, for fifty years. He is a legendary boxing trainer in Ireland, having taught at the Olympic Boxing Club for thirty-five years, and trained champions Francis Barrett, Ruchan Heaney, Michael John Heffernan and Seán Harty. Chick is married to Maureen Gillen, who is originally from Dublin, and they have six children, Linda, Ann, Gloria, Michael, Patrick and Paddy Farrell, and twelve grandchildren. Chick enjoys going to race meetings, playing pitch-and-toss, and, of course, boxing.

Galway

Chick Gillen

'In my life as a barber, I have seen many young lads who had their first haircut from me come back with their sons, and even grandsons, to have their first haircuts. I have seen lots of young men return from distant places, successful, yet still returning to Chick's in Dominick Street. I recall a man returning after a fifty-year absence from Ireland. I had given him his parting haircut all those years ago when he was leaving to make a new life in Australia.

Many come for a haircut for that important interview or promotion, and I like to think that I played a part in their success, however small. I even supplied a young chap with a suit for his interview, a suit my son had worn for his brother's wedding that he no longer needed. Needless to say, he got the job.

I like to think of myself as a cosmopolitan barber, in that I have visitors from all over the world. My only condition is that they send a postcard on their return home. One young lad, on holiday from New Zealand, popped his head in one day inquiring about the price of a haircut, saying he had very little money. I couldn't refuse him and jokingly said, "Sure you can send me the money" – and he did! My philosophy in life is this: Work like you don't need the money, love like you've never been hurt, and dance like nobody's watching you!'

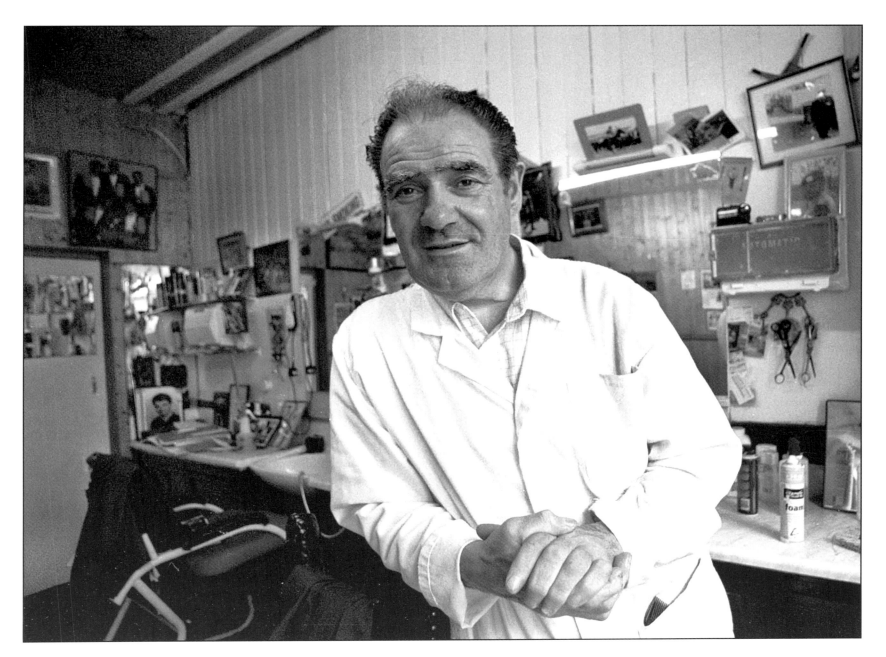

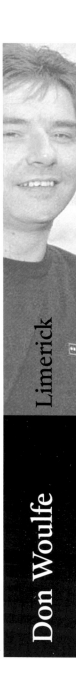

Limerick

Don Woulfe

Don Woulfe is a plumber working in the construction industry in Dublin city, installing plumbing devices in new housing developments. Originally from Limerick city, he is a former pupil of St Munchin's College, Limerick. He began his apprenticeship in plumbing after leaving school. He now lives in Clonee, County Meath, with his wife Colette Dower. Don's family includes his mother Celine and brothers Nicholas and Ciarán. Sadly, both his father Mick and his brother Michael are now deceased. Don's passion in life is rugby. He has played with St Munchin's College and Thomond and Shannon Rugby Clubs, and he is a current member of Ashborne Rugby Club. Don really enjoyed Munster's European Cup journey in the 1999 season. He also enjoys soccer. Both Don and Colette are the proud owners of Squitcher the cat, Woody the rabbit and Dustin the cockatiel!

'For all the times in my life when things didn't seem to be going the way I wanted; for the ups and downs, the highs and lows, the pain and the sorrow; for all the moments I despaired and felt life was being unfair to me, I now know that during all the things life has put before me, I was on a journey, but I was never alone.'

Footprints

One night a man had a dream. He dreamed he was walking along the beach with the Lord. Across the sky flashed scenes from his life. For each scene, he noticed two sets of footprints in the sand; one belonging to him, and the other to the Lord.

When the last scene of his life flashed before him, he looked back at the footprints in the sand. He noticed that many times along the path of his life there was only one set of footprints. He also noticed that it happened at the very lowest and saddest times in his life.

This really bothered him and he questioned the Lord about it. 'Lord, you said that once I decided to follow you, you'd walk with me all the way. But I have noticed that during the most troublesome times in my life, there is only one set of footprints. I don't understand why when I needed you most you would leave me.'

The Lord replied, 'My son, my precious child, I love you and I would never leave you. During your times of trial and suffering, when you see only one set of footprints, it was then that I carried you.'

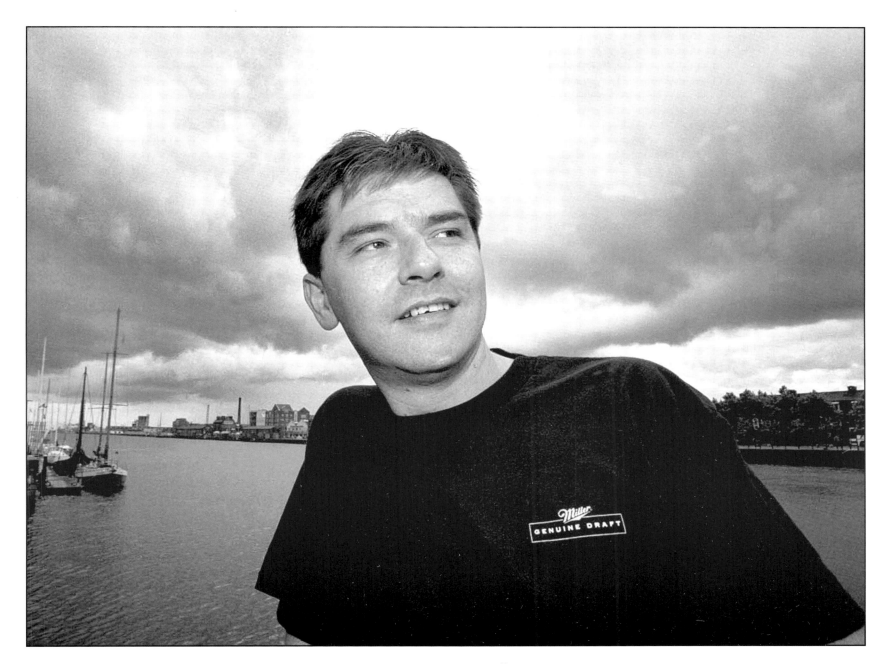

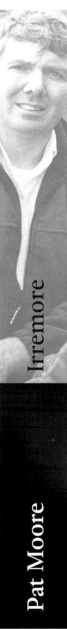

Pat Moore is a priest in Irremore, Lixnaw, which is a village in north Kerry. He has been working there for three years. Previously, he worked in Gneeveguilla, east Kerry. Pat went to school in his native Asdee, and subsequently to Maynooth College and Rome. He is deeply conscious of the role of the priest in the local community. Since surviving a serious illness, he has appreciated more the outdoor life and the company of friends. Pat has two brothers, Diarmuid and Michael, who are both married. Pat's mother, Peg, still lives in the family home in Asdee. Tom is also an accomplished writer and broadcaster, and is a trustee of 'A Day in the Bog', a local community project near Listowel town.

'Working with an ageing community, I find myself increasingly involved in the lead-up to people's obsequies. The image I find myself relying on at that time, as human experience is harrowed for the planting of the Paschal Mystery, is the image of the individual being like a river flowing towards the sea. Just as the river is absorbed into the ocean, so also do we, at death, when time and space dissolve, become absorbed into the great sea of God. I have chosen an old prayer that I find very helpful to inhabit at this time.'

Go forth upon your journey, from this world, O Christian Soul,
In the name of God, the almighty Father, who created you
In the name of Jesus, his son, who redeemed you,
In the name of the Holy Spirit, who sanctifies you.
May your Guardian Angel support and defend you,
May the prayers of the saints help you
May Jesus look upon you with pardon and mercy
May you have peace as you rest with Jesus this day in paradise
Depart, O Christian Soul, out of this world.

Pat Moore stands at the edge of Ballybunion's cliff face, where the river Shannon is absorbed into the ocean

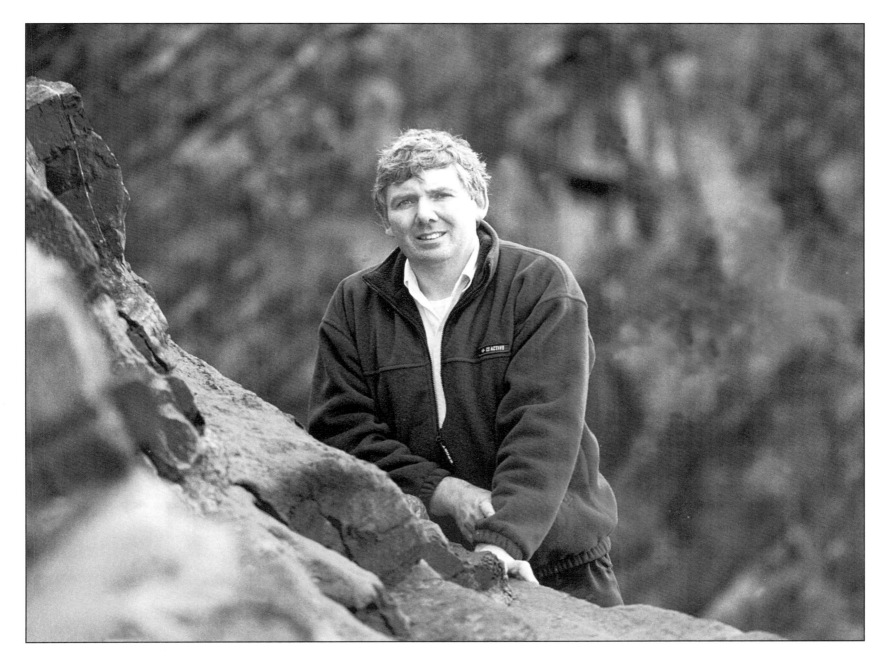

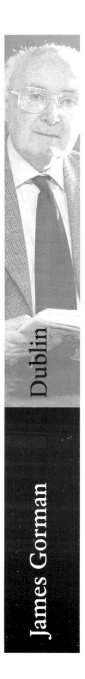

James Gorman has recently graduated as a mature student from Trinity College, Dublin. He completed an M.Litt., translating and editing an unpublished fourteenth-century Latin manuscript from the college library. Born in Scotland, where his parents had moved for a short while, James is a retired business executive. His wife, Mary, died last year. James has three daughters, Freda, Angela and Patricia, and four grandchildren. He is a keen golfer, enjoys reading history, is a member of the Dublin Rotary Club, and has been a member of Neighbourhood Watch for twelve years in his area. Much travelled until recently, he has discovered the charms of keeping close to home.

Stay, stay at home at rest;
Homekeeping hearts are happiest.
For those that wander they know not where
Are full of trouble and full of care.
To stay at home is best.

Anon.

What canst thou see elsewhere which thou seest not here?
Behold the heavens and the earth, and all the elements;
for of these are all things made.

from *The Imitation of Christ* by Thomas à Kempis (1379–1471)

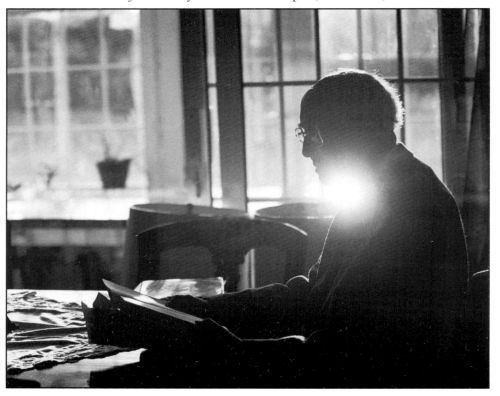

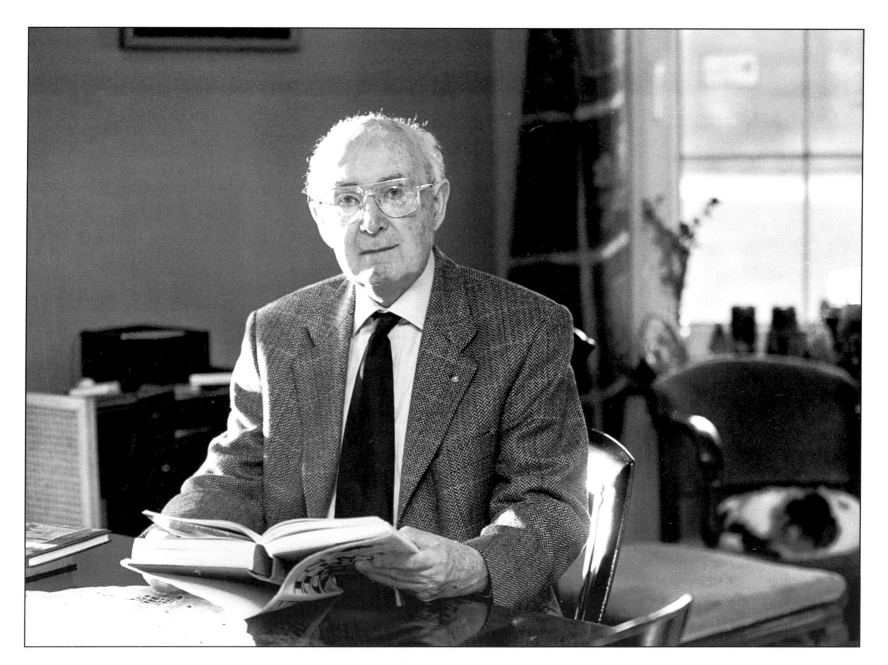

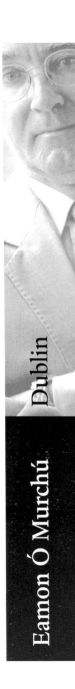

Eamon Ó Murchú Dublin

Eamon Ó Murchú has been the principal of Scoil Chiaráin in Glasnevin for thirty years. It is a school for special needs, in the parish of Ballygall. Eamon has taught all his working life and has written extensively on the need for special education in Ireland. Originally from Listowel, County Kerry, Eamon is married to Nora Ní Loideáin from Connemara, and they have three children, Clíodhna, Nuala and Deirdre. Eamon has a passion for Irish language and culture and the writings of past and present Kerry authors, in particular, the literature of Bryan McMahon. His hobbies include theatre, photography, cycling, reading, and poetry.

'**Thank you** for my father for his love of family, sense of place, gift of words and service to community.

Thank you for my mother for her unconditional love and unfailing good humour.

Thank you for my master who taught me about the uniqueness of each individual human being, and the importance of the celebration of diversity among humankind.

Thank you for the priest who, through his own scholarship and refined dignity, filled me with a pride in the tradition of the primary teacher in Ireland.

Thank you for the priest and best friend who was the humblest of men and the living and godly expression of community in action.

Thank you for the brother who stepped in when everybody else stepped out.

Thank you for the old man who proved to me that the most learned of men need never go to school, and that the most important learning of all is that which we receive at the hearth.

Thank you for the Corkman who proved to me that vision, when coupled with passion and commitment, can realise the impossible.

Thank you for the Kerryman whose inspired leadership generated a great pride in my profession.

Thank you for the nun who continues to teach me about love, vocation, prayer and grace.

Thank you for my own special place where I can reflect, renew and re-create.

Thank you for three daughters who continue to live, love and laugh with me.

Thank you for the son I never had who continues to have a tincture with me.

Thank you for my best friend and for the love she continues to give me generously.

Thank you, Lord, for these your gifts, which continue to give voice and direction to my teaching.'

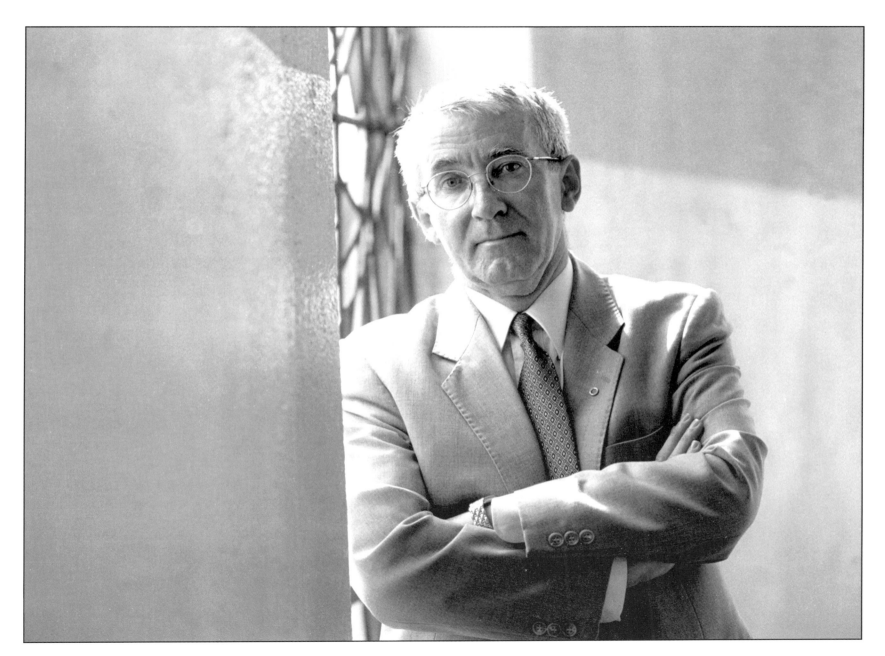

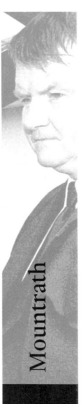

Seamus Burke is an undertaker and auctioneer in Mountrath, County Laois. He carries on a business that has been in the Burke family for forty-nine years, and handles about thirty-five funerals each year. A native of Mountrath, Seamus is married to Mary Theresa and they have three children, Sarah, Aoife and Tadhg. His mother Lil and uncle Johnny Burke still work in the family business. Seamus enjoys all GAA sports, especially hurling and football, and also enjoys eating out and the company of good friends.

'My own sister Mary died just over a year ago. She was only forty-six years old and left behind her husband Brian Kelly and their young twins. I can really understand what people are going through in bereavement, especially since her untimely death. As an undertaker in a small town you tend to know every person; everyone is related, so it's not just a job for me, it's much more. I try to make their grief a little less painful. It makes the funeral much more personal. Death is never easy at any time.'

Lord, let me make this day easy for these people who are grieving today.

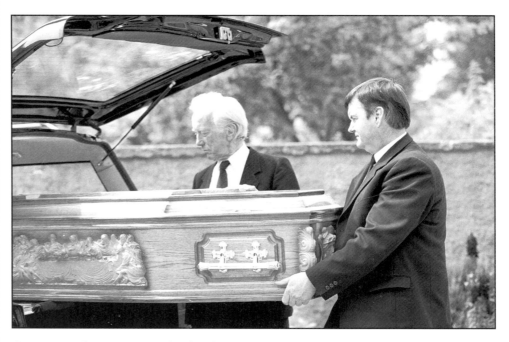

Seamus Burke carries on the family's undertaking business, which has been in the family for forty-nine years. His uncle Johnny Burke (also pictured) assists him with all the funerals.

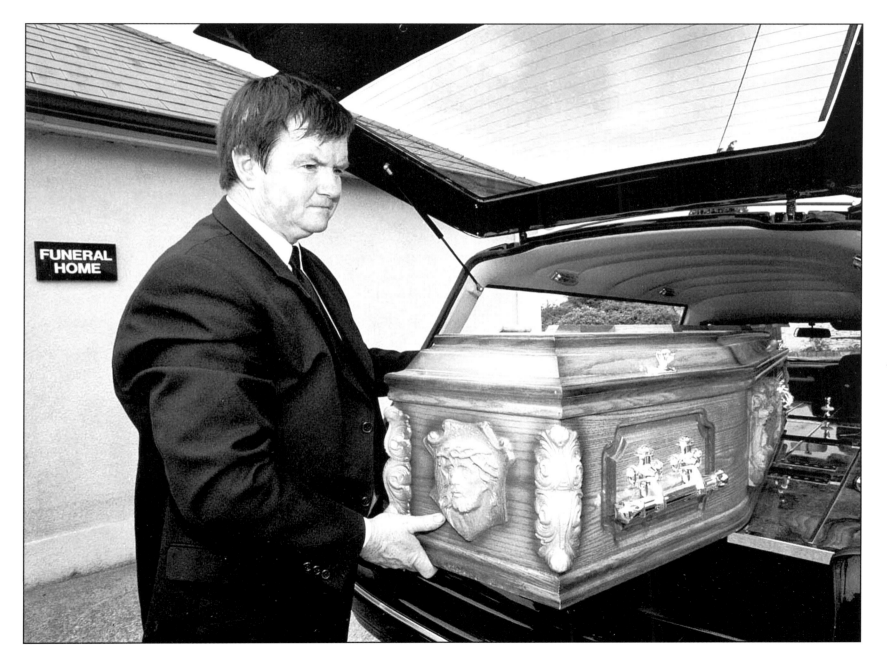

Dublin

Ryan Tubridy

Ryan Tubridy is a radio presenter/ broadcaster and reporter with RTÉ. He started his career with the station at the age of twelve, reviewing books on *Poporama*. At UCD, he studied the history of Greek and Roman civilisation. He works as a roving reporter with *The Pat Kenny Show* and Myles Dungan's *5–7 Live*, and also presents *The Sunday Show* on RTÉ Radio One. Originally from Blackrock, County Dublin, he now lives in Drimnagh with his partner Ann-marie and their baby daughter Ella Catherine. His own family includes parents Pat and Catherine, and sisters and brothers Judith, Niall, Rachael and Garrett. Ryan enjoys the music of crooner Frank Sinatra, watching old monochrome films and *Inspector Morse*, walking by Avondale, Rathdrum, with a flask of coffee and a good book, and fly fishing in Galway, but most of all he loves his job.

Advent

We have tested and tasted too much, lover –
Through a chink too wide there comes in no wonder.
But here in this Advent-darkened room
Where the dry black bread and the sugarless tea
Of penance will charm back the luxury
Of a child's soul, we'll return to Doom
The knowledge we stole but could not use

And for the newness that was in every stale thing
When we looked at it as children: the spirit-shocking
Wonder in a black slanting Ulster hill
Or the prophetic astonishment in the tedious talking
Of an old fool will awake for us and bring
You and me to the yard gate to watch the whins
And the bog-holes, cart-tracks, old stables where Time begins.

O after Christmas we'll have no need to go searching
For the difference that sets an old phrase buring –
We'll hear it in the whispered argument of a churning
Or in the streets where the village boys are lurching.
And we'll hear it among simple decent men too
Who barrow dung in gardens under trees,
Wherever life pours ordinary plenty.
Won't we be rich, my love and I, and please
God we shall not ask for reason's payment,
The why of heart-breaking strangeness in dreeping hedges
Nor analyse God's breath in common statement.
We have thrown into the dust-bin the clay-minted wages
Of pleasure, knowledge and the conscious hour –
And Christ comes with a January flower.

Patrick Kavanagh (1904–67)

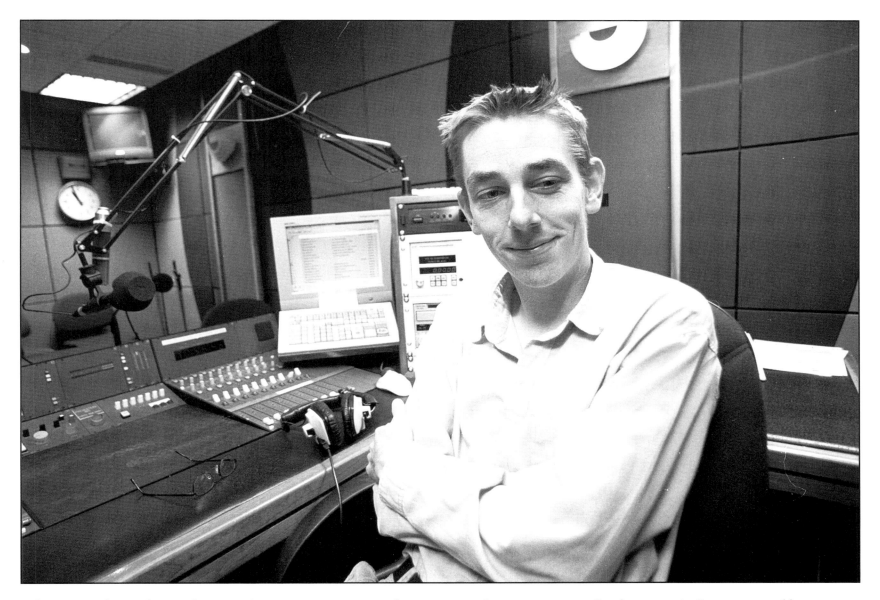

'The reason I chose 'Advent' is because it's as innocent as it is simple. For me it tends to conjure up smells of cut grass in Connemara and hot car-seats in mid-July; childhood – uncomplicated and fun.'

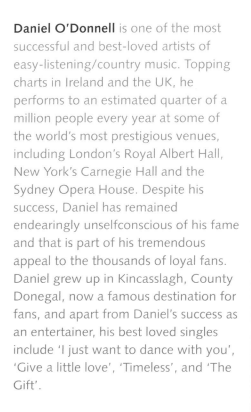

Daniel O'Donnell is one of the most successful and best-loved artists of easy-listening/country music. Topping charts in Ireland and the UK, he performs to an estimated quarter of a million people every year at some of the world's most prestigious venues, including London's Royal Albert Hall, New York's Carnegie Hall and the Sydney Opera House. Despite his success, Daniel has remained endearingly unselfconscious of his fame and that is part of his tremendous appeal to the thousands of loyal fans. Daniel grew up in Kincasslagh, County Donegal, now a famous destination for fans, and apart from Daniel's success as an entertainer, his best loved singles include 'I just want to dance with you', 'Give a little love', 'Timeless', and 'The Gift'.

Daniel is at the very heart of the Romanian Challenge Appeal, which was formed in 1990, and he has helped raise close to a million pounds for the appeal through fund-raising. He has also set up Kincasslagh House and Neptune house, which are houses for those forgotten orphans whose life before this was lived out in rat-infested dark cold orphanages, where children lay undernourished and seriously ill.

'You've seen the faces of the children in the houses and the joy, so you know it has been worthwhile. I get emotional, not at the horror of the institution but when I visit the homes. You see the happiness and the hope, and remember the children left behind.'

Yesterday's a memory,
tomorrow's a mystery
today is a gift
that's why they call it the present.

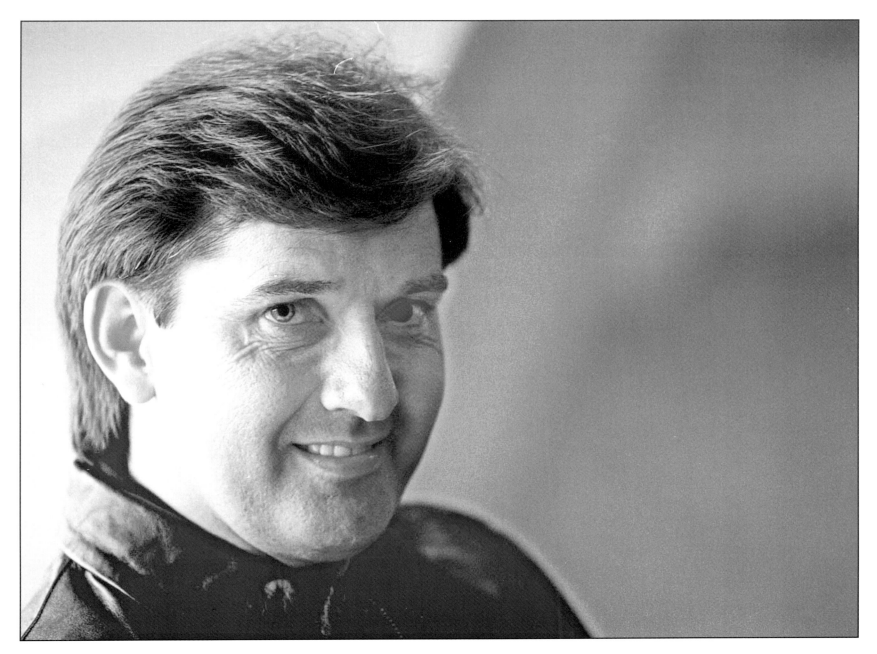

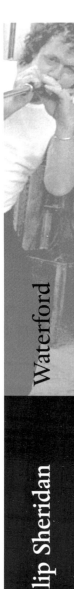

Philip (Skippy) Sheridan is a master blower at Waterford Crystal, a company celebrated world-wide for its individuality in handcrafted glass design. Philip started his apprenticeship with the company in 1969. He uses the ancient art of glass-blowing to mould Waterford Crystal's flagship Claret decanters, trophies and chandeliers. A native of Waterford City, Philip is married to Patricia and they have four children, Lee, Donna, Mark and Laura. He plays percussion in many Waterford bands, and enjoys music and cycling.

'Since I started in 1969, technology has changed so much, and yet, on reflection, we held onto our own handcraft, using the ancient materials, bits of wood, bits of stick, bits of paper, and lots of skill! Luckily, it's 60 per cent inspiration and 40 per cent perspiration. With the art of blowing you can really express yourself and put your own ideas into the piece. That's what art is all about. You must have a healthy respect for hot metal and be in control of it all the time. On a spiritual level, the craft I use is a gift, and hopefully I can pass it on to someone to keep the adventure going. Technology must never outstrip handcrafts. It is a beautiful art form. We see our finished art in cathedrals around the world, in the Vatican and many fine houses, and, believe it or not, many of the employers will often ask us to make water fonts and prayer books.'

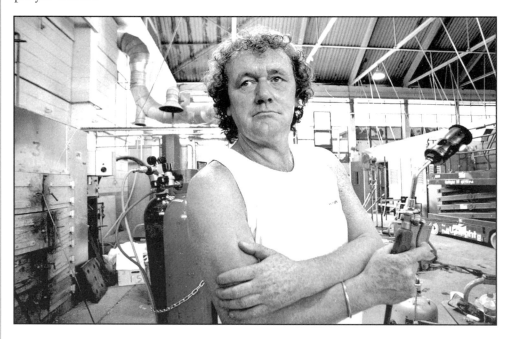

'It's tough work, passionate, and probably the only job in the world where the harder you try, the worse it gets. Glass has a mind of its own.'

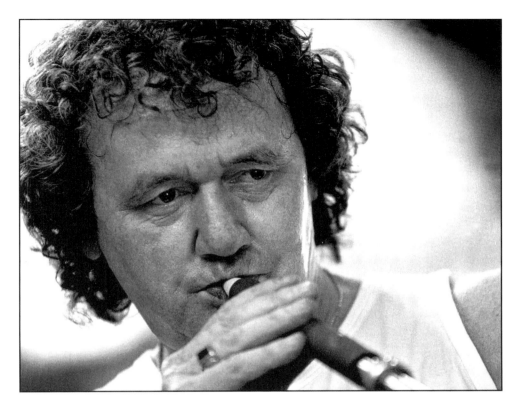
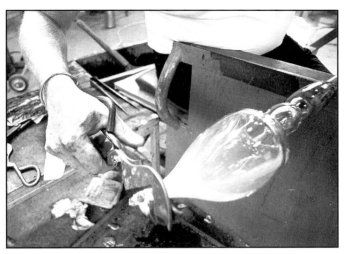
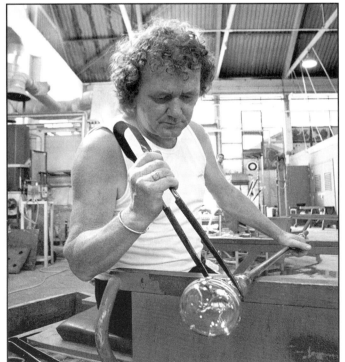
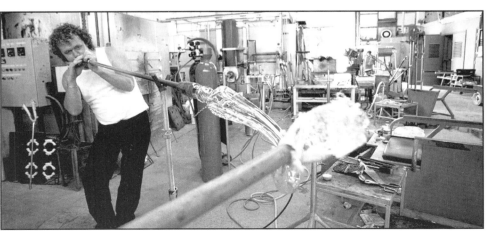

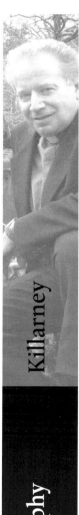

Bill Murphy is Bishop of the Diocese of Kerry. He was ordained Bishop in 1995. Prior to that he was administrator of the parish of Killarney and was the first director of the John Paul II Pastoral Centre in the town. He was born in Annaghmore, Glenflesk, and studied for the priesthood at Maynooth College. He was ordained in 1961 and taught for six years at St Colman's College, Newry, and then studied catechetics at Lumen Vitae, Brussels, and Fordham University, New York. Bishop Murphy spent three years at the Gregorian University, Rome, where he was awarded a Doctorate in Divinity in 1973. He worked with the primary catechetical commission preparing the *Children of God* series, and taught theology in the Institute for Religious Education, Mount Oliver, Dundalk, before returning to Kerry in 1979 as diocesan director of religious education in post-primary schools, and co-ordinator of adult religious education in the diocese. His family includes his brother Archdeacon Michael Murphy and sisters Tessie, Ann, Sr Therese and Mary (Sr Marie and his brother Daniel are deceased). He enjoys hillwalking, reading and travel.

'I will write about my favourite time for prayer rather than my favourite prayer. I would love to be able to say that I always find prayer easy, but I don't. For me, prayer comes easiest in the early morning. I live in Killarney, near St Mary's Cathedral on the edge of the national park. When weather permits, which it generally does, I take an early morning walk in Knockreer Estate. As I walk along the Deenagh river, I can easily identify with Patrick Kavanagh's "Ploughman":

> *Tranquillity walks with me*
> *And no care.*
> *O, the quiet ecstasy*
> *Like a prayer.*

Pugin's Cathedral in the background, the majestic McGillicuddy Reeks and the Tomies out in front, the surrounding woodlands, the colourful flowers, the sound of the river, the stillness of Lough Lein, the singing of the birds – all these bring life to the words of Elizabeth Barrett Browning (1806–1861):

> *Earth's crammed with heaven,*
> *And every common bush afire with God;*
> *But only he who sees, takes off his shoes...*

Very often I pray the psalms of the breviary as I walk along, and I try to remember that I am walking in an area hallowed by centuries of prayer. Within view are the ruins of Innisfallen, a monastic site and centre of learning for a thousand years; Aghadoe, where monastic life flourished as early as the fifth century; and Muckross Abbey, home to Observantine Franciscans from the fiftheenth to the seventeenth century. I am conscious that the psalms I am saying in English were chanted in Latin by the monks who once inhabited these ruins.

Linking up with this rich Christian heritage gives me a sense of belonging to something great and noble and helps me to put present happenings in the Church and in the world in perspective.'

O Lord, I love the house in which you dwell, and the place where your glory abides.

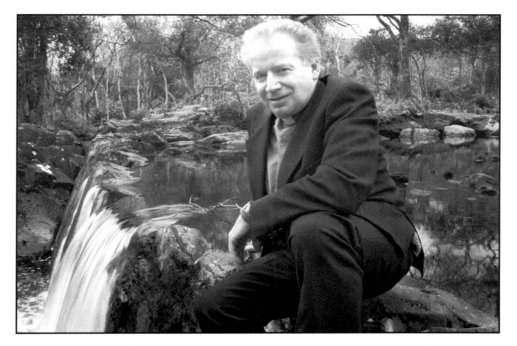

Meeting the stranger... Bill Murphy chats to Perenton from Nigeria as they make the assent up Mount Brandon, County Kerry, to celebrate St Brendan's Day.

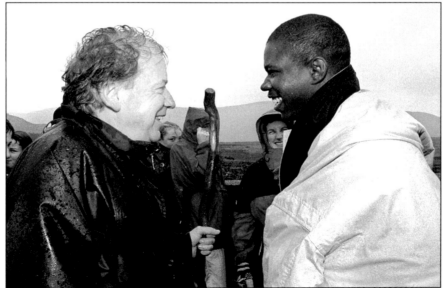

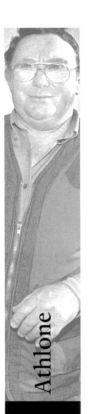

Percy Hewitt has recently retired, after forty-eight years as lock-keeper at Shannon lock. Carrying on a family tradition since his grandfather William in 1867, his son Robert will now carry the work on into this century. The Hewitts have lived in the lock-house since 1900. As well as opening and closing the famous lock, they collect tolls and keep accounts. In 1900 it cost 1/6 to pass through the lock. Today it costs £1.20. Percy has two daughters, Cindy and Vicky, as well as Robert, who is also a member of an up-and-coming rock band, Murv. Percy enjoys fishing in the west of Ireland, tennis, and badminton, and has played on the inter-provincial Connacht badminton team.

'Since 1867, through three generations, the Hewitt's have manned the lock in Athlone. Robert, my son, is currently carrying the name into the twenty-first century. I took over the baton from my late father in August 1952, and, up to retiring in May 2000, had the pleasure of meeting many people of different cultures and creeds.

Looking back on my life, I have enjoyed working around water. Fond childhood memories that come to mind include being allowed to pilot a canal barge into my dad's lock. The barge skippers were the salt of the earth. I always loved fishing and could catch some for tea in a matter of minutes at that time. In 1959, with the introduction of road and rail transport, which challenged barge power, the Shannon almost ground to a halt. It was only a handful of private boats that kept the river open.

In 1961–2, the Shannon came to life again with the introduction of the leisure craft, and has gone from strength to strength since. Twelve thousand crafts or more use the lock annually at present. Only God knows what the numbers will rise to in the coming years.'

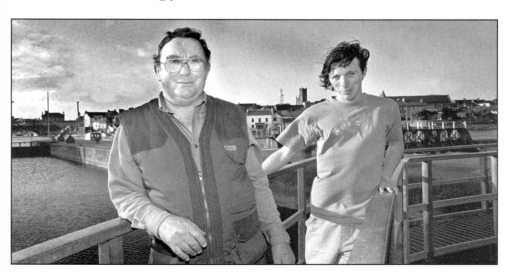

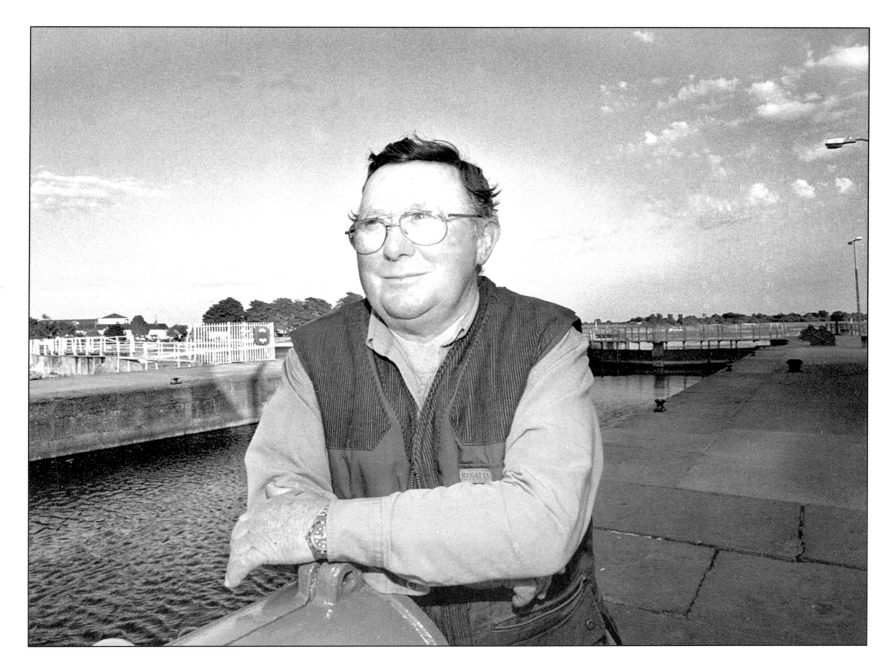

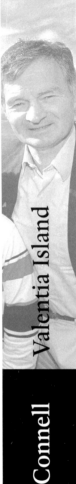

Valentia Island

Michael O'Connell

Mick O'Connell is a true Islander, at home with the sea, his family, the island community and the Kerry coast. He is considered to be one of the most skilful and talented midfield players of all time. Born on Beginish Island in 1937, Mick played for Kerry minors in 1955 and for the seniors in 1956. Playing in a total of ten All-Ireland Senior Football Championship finals, he has won four All-Ireland Sam Maguire cup medals, and, in 1959, Mick captained the Kingdom to a 3-7 victory over Galway. He has also won six National Football league winner's medals. His solitary Railway cup medal came at the age of thirty-five in the 1972 final against Leinster.

Mick worked with the Western Union Telegraph Company on the Island until its closure in 1966. He is both a fisherman and farmer on the island. Mick is married to Rosaleen, who is from Cavan, and they have three children, Maura, Michael and Diarmuid. Both Mick and Rosaleen have donated a site on the island for a new residential centre developed for people with learning disabilities. In 1999, Michael was awarded the prestigious Kerry Person of the Year award, which recognised his contribution to Kerry life, not only as a footballer, but as a man prepared to give his time to so many worthy causes, especially The Kerry Parents and Friends Association.

Count your every blessings
And name them one by one
And then it will surprise you
At what the Lord has done.

'I count myself very lucky to have been born on Valentia Island on the edge of the Atlantic, with family roots centuries old. In health, family and with neighbours, and with a bit of sport thrown in, life has been good to me. I too have many reasons to thank the Lord.'

Mick O'Connell is pictured with his wife Rosaleen and son Diarmuid on Valentia Island

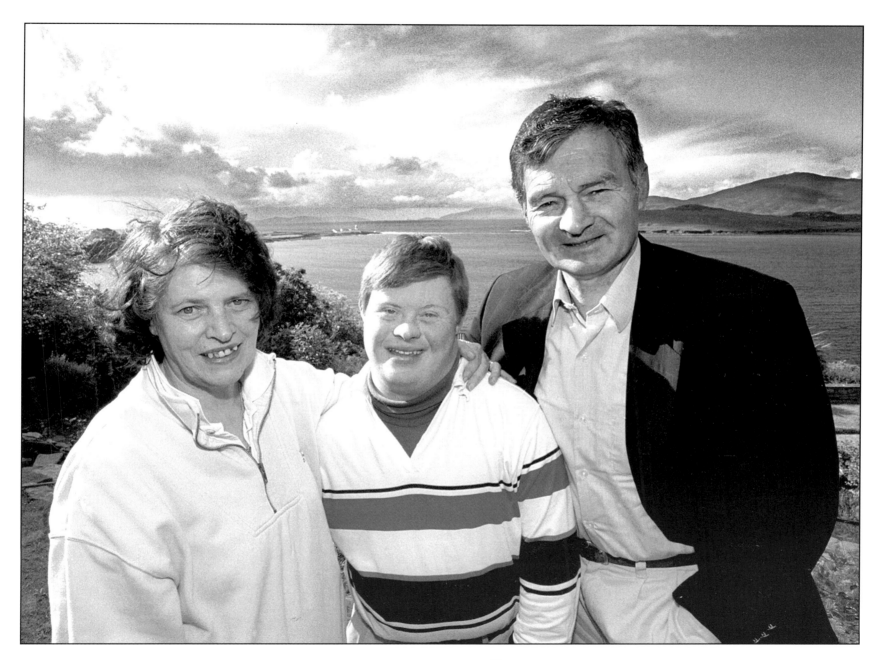

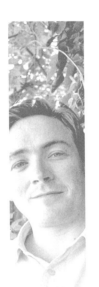

Michael McGlynn

Michael McGlynn is a composer and founder of the world-renowned chamber choir Anúna, best known internationally as the originators of the choral sound and image of the phenomenally successful Riverdance. Michael has recorded seven albums with the group. His compositional style is a unique blend of the ancient and modern, combining the different formal structures of medieval and contemporary.

Michael was born in Dublin and is married to Lucy Champion. His twin brother John is the Production Designer with Anúna and Michael's other brother Tom also performs with the group. Michael enjoys swimming, gardening, reading, sailing, fishing, astronomy, and Irish and English medieval literature.

'I studied Francis Ledwidge and his poetry at school, but it was through the work of Liam O'Meara and his book *The Complete Poems of Francis Ledwidge* that I became aware of the many similarities that exist between Ledwidge and my own compositions. Indeed, one of the reasons I studied English with music was the link between the two art forms. Music is a strange thing; it exists only for the moment that the sound is heard, and yet has a resonance that can change our lives. The composer puts a unique stamp on a lyric – rarely, however, more beautiful than in *Les Illuminations*, the music of Benjamin Britten allied to the work of Arthur Rimbaud, something that composers like myself can only aspire to. Ledwidge died in the First World War, but his poetry remains as fresh today as it must have been then. The poetry is pastoral and often nostalgic, but the truth behind its simplicity is often as deep as that of the early poetry that I have set for Anúna.

A fine example of his work is 'A Soldier's Grave', which is self-explanatory. I set this as the song 'Midnight' on the Anúna album *Behind the Closed Eye* (1997), an album also featuring the Ulster Orchestra that explores Ledwidge's work and my own reaction to it.'

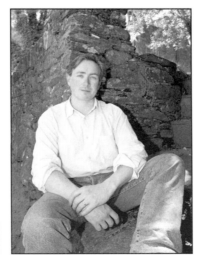

A Soldier's Grave

Then in the lull of midnight, gentle arms
Lifted him slowly down the slopes of death,
Lest he should hear again the mad alarms
Of battle, dying moans, and painful breath.

And where the earth was soft for flowers we made
A grave for him that he might better rest.,
So, Spring shall come and leave it sweet arrayed,
And there the lark shall turn her dewy nest.

Francis Ledwidge (1891–1917)

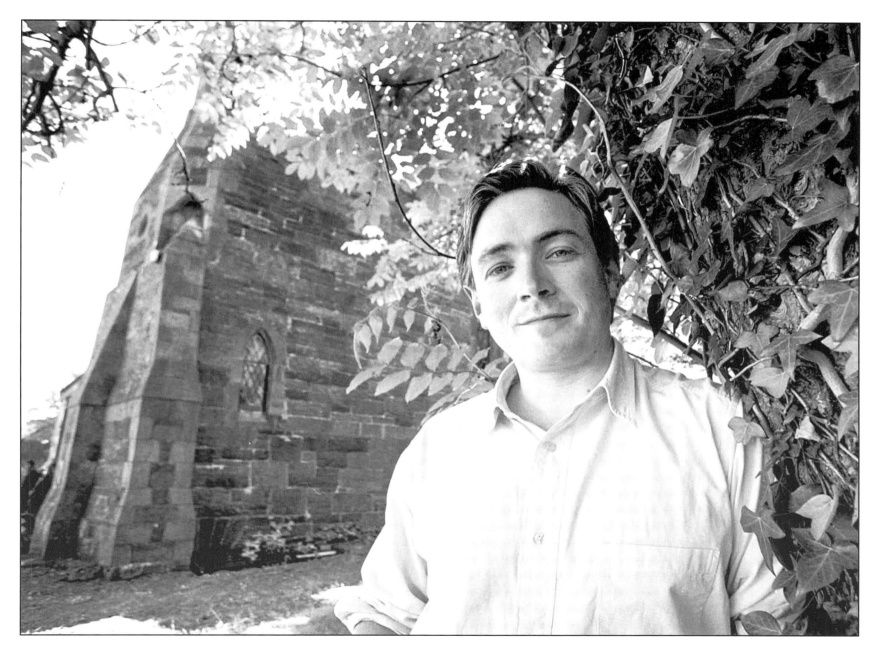

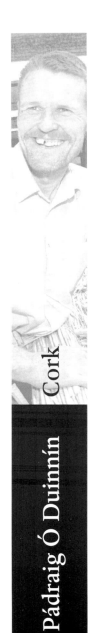

Pádraig Ó Duinnín is a traditional boat builder at Meitheal Mara, which is based in Crosses Green House, Cork City. Meitheal Mara is a company dedicated to the development and education, through community enterprise, of the marine culture of Ireland. Pádraig trains people in the ancient craft of making currachs and coracles, which have been associated with Celtic voyaging for thousands of years. The most famous of these skin-covered boats is that of St Brendan, in which he travelled to the 'New World'. Meitheal Mara specialise in building the Naomhóg (west Kerry currach), the Sheephaven Currach (Donegal), the Aran Islands Currach, the Boyne Coracle Currach (Mayo), the Belderrig Currach (Cork), and the Cummeenatrush log-boat. They also produce an old maritime map of Cork and sea chests. Pádraig is from Coolcower in Macroom, County Cork. Prior to his involvement with Meitheal Mara he was a civil engineer.

He is married to Claire Ní Mhuirthile and they have three children, Siobhán, Cáit and Seán. Pádraig enjoys Irish folk music and the traditional folk cultures of other countries.

Togáil Bád

'Múnlaíonn tú soitheach ionas go mbeidh sé socair ar snámh, slán ós na tonntracha agus fuirist le brú tríd an uisce.

Cuimhníonn tú ar na daoine a bheidh ar bharr na huiscí doimhneacha agus glacann tú leis an mhuinín atá acu as do cheard agus as ceard na saortha a d'imigh romhainn.

Ag an láinseáil guíonn tú go dtarraingeóidh na bádóirí le chéile agus go dtiocfaidh siad slán ó gach baol a bhaineann le bheith ar a bhfarraige.

Le cúnamh Dé.'

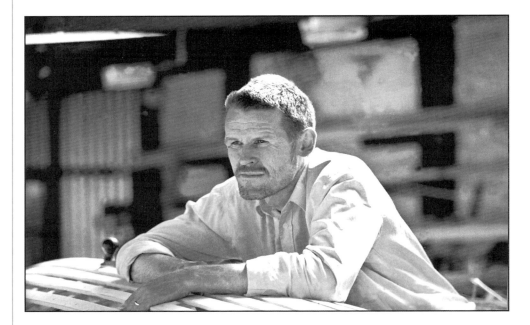

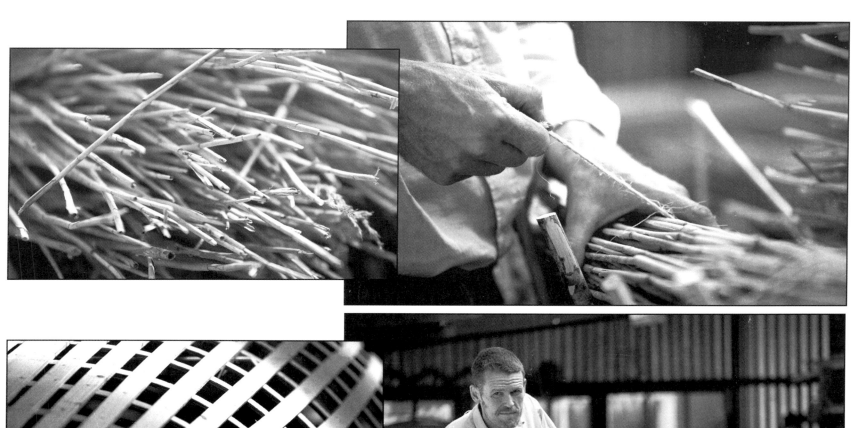

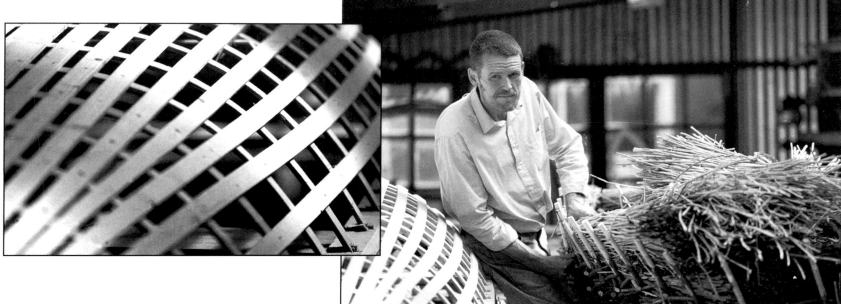

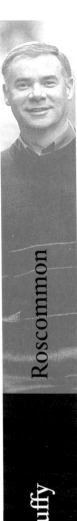

Eugene Duffy is Director of the Western Theological Institute in Galway, which provides theological resources for the six Roman Catholic dioceses in the western province. Apart from administrative work, Eugene teaches theology at NUI Galway, the Galway-Mayo Institute of Technology, and St Angela's College, Sligo. Eugene also works with clergy and catechists, providing ongoing education and renewal programmes in theology and related disciplines. From 1980 to 1982 Eugene was a curate in Killavil in County Sligo, and then returned to Maynooth for further studies until 1985. During this time he acted as Junior Dean in the College. He also taught theology at All Hallows College, Dubin, where he was Head of the Department of Systematic Theology and Director of Formation for seminarians.

He was offered a visiting scholarship to Boston College, and, in 1997, he was awarded a doctorate by the Milltown Institute of Theology and Philosophy. Eugene's mother Eileen still lives in the family home near Ballaghaderreen, County Roscommon. He has one sister Marian and one brother John. Eugene's hobbies include reading, hillwalking and travel.

'A quiet walk in the countryside can be for me a genuinely spiritual experience. It was in the midst of nature, too, that the psalmist found overtures of God's presence in the world.

You made the moon to mark the months,
the sun knows the time for its setting.
When you spread darkness it is night,
and all the beasts of the forest creep forth.
The young lions roar for their prey,
and ask their food from God.

At the rising of the sun they steal away,
and go to rest in their dens.
Man goes forth to his work, to labour till evening falls.
How many are your works, O Lord!
In wisdom you have made them all.
The earth is full of your riches.

Psalm 103 (104): 19-24

The same sense of awe before the grandeur of God's creation has pervaded Irish religious poetry from its earliest days. It is still a feature of the work of contemporary religious poets; I find it well expressed in "A Thought From Hildegard" by Pádraig J. Daly, who senses the hints of transcendence in features of the countryside, both ancient and new.'

A Thought From Hildegard

Butterflies are going from flower to flower,
Bees work drivenly among the marigolds,
Blackbirds bathe in a trickle of water.

The pines sway lightly in the summer breeze,
A lime rustles with enormous gentleness,
Thistledown floats by on the air.

Cars make their way along the valley,
An empty train passes,
An aeroplane drifts patiently across the sky.

I worship Him
Who wears this green and movement as a coat.

from *The Voice of the Hare* (1997)
by Pádraig J. Daly (b. 1943)

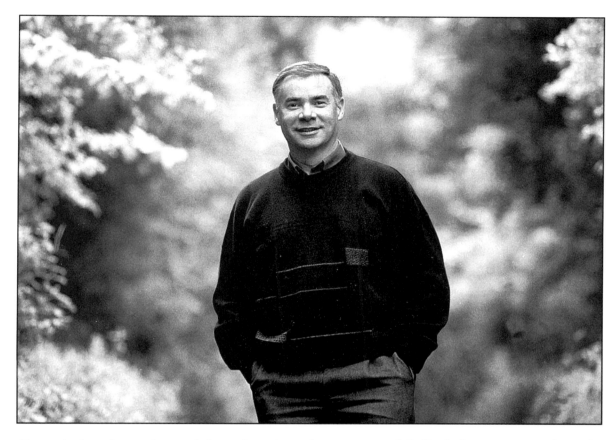

'For me both psalms and poetry help to give voice to the experience of God's abiding presence in the midst of creation.'

Lieutenant Commander Paul O'Connell is Able Seaman and Ship's Gunner on board the L.E. Roisín. He joined the Irish Navy in February 1999. Paul received the Best Recruit Award 2000, which is sponsored by the organisation of ex-servicemen and women. General duties for Paul on board the L.E. Roisín include helmsman, ship's security, ship's deck maintenance, sea rider, coxswain, and a member of the guns crew on the 20mm ship's secondary armament on board. Paul is from Commons Road in Cork city. His family includes his mother Catherine, brother John and sister Michelle. Paul is a member of Na Piarsaigh GAA Club and plays hurling, gaelic football and soccer.

They that go down to the sea in ships: and occupy their business in great waters; these see the works of the Lord and his wonders of the deep.

from Psalm 107

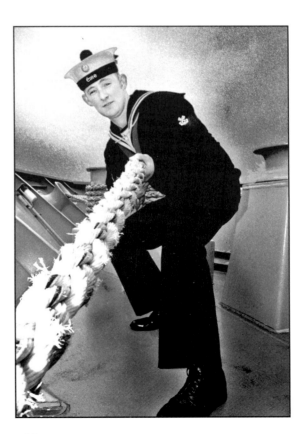

Lt Cdr Paul O'Connell on board the L.E. Roisín

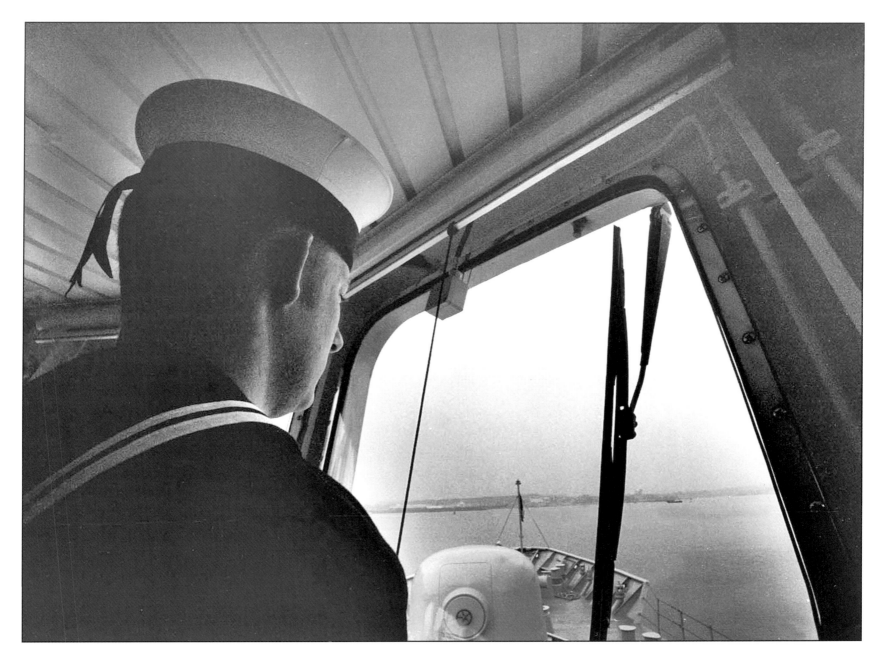

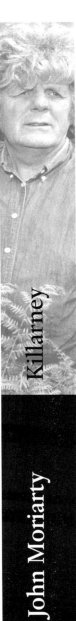

Killarney

John Moriarty

Living as he does in the mountains in Coolies, **John Moriarty** lives outside the modern consensus about the world. Originally from Moyvane in north Kerry, John studied at University College Dublin, then was tutor in Leeds University and subsequently lectured in English Literature at the University of Manitoba in Canada for six years. He returned to Ireland and lived and worked as a gardener in Connemara for twenty years, three of which were spent in solitude. John returned to his native Kerry five years ago.

His many books and volumes include *Dreamtime, Turtle has gone a long time* (3 volumes), and his autobiography, entitled *Nostos*, which will be published by The Lilliput Press in 2001. John's family includes his brother Chris and sisters Madeleine, Babs, Brenda and Phyllis. John is passionate about nature and its mountains and rivers. He enjoys the company of his neighbours and friends, and by way of distraction he enjoys watching sport.

'Now at sixty two, looking back on my life, my baptism is undoubtedly the greatest thing that has happened to me, my baptism into the passion, death and resurrection of Christ. Most of my life is an attempt to have full ascendancy over me and in me. In this I am thinking of Romans 6:3-4.

> *Know ye not, that so many of us were baptised into Jesus Christ, were baptised into his death? Therefore we are buried with him by baptism into death: that like as Christ was raised up from the dead by the glory of the Father, even so we also should walk in the newness of life.*

One of the great wonders to me is the great Paschal candle from which my baptismal candle was lighted. It was there at my cradle lighting my way through life, and will I hope be there by my coffin lighting my way in the hereafter.

What we are talking about here is the wounded *lumen christi*, the light of Christ with the five nails driven into it. Because it is a wounded light, it will also be a compassionate light – that compassion I need. My hope is that that compassionate guiding light will go before me always.'

John Moriarty with with the Mountains of Torc and Mongerton in the background

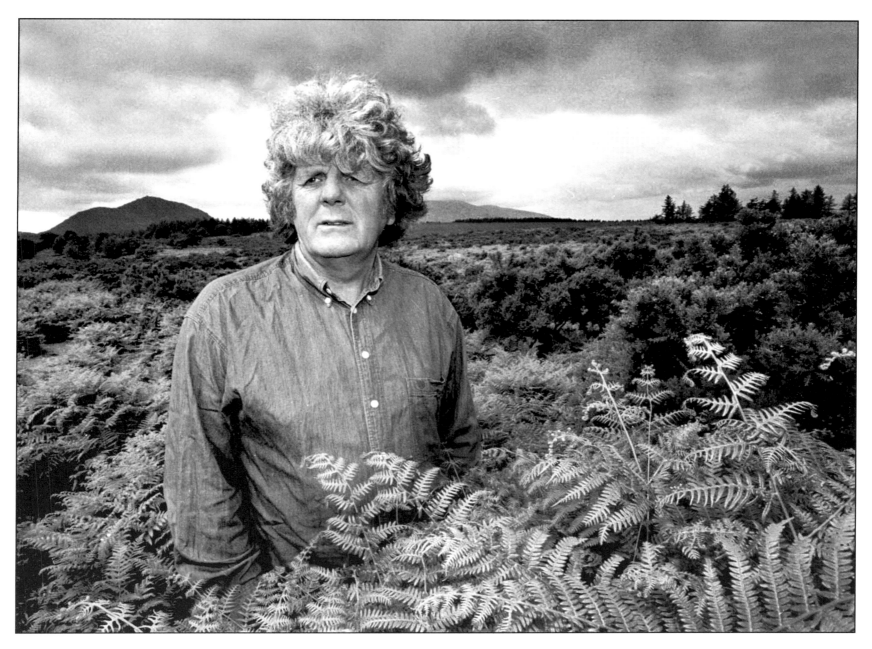

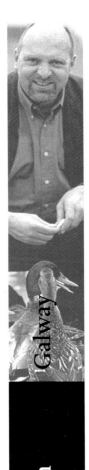

Joe Coughlan

Joe Couglan is a residential child-care manager with the Western Health Board, working with adolescents who are in care. Prior to that he worked as a social educator, social researcher and home/school liaison officer. Joe also runs Woodquays newsagent, which is in the heart of Galway city and has been in the family for generations. Joe is married to Gillian Gillen from Sligo and they have two children, Katie and Eoin. Joe is a National League basketball coach, winning three national titles with the Sligo All-Stars, Kerry Spring and Moycullen. He also enjoys hillwalking, cycling and photography.

'It is my belief that we must respect other people's experience and all they have done for us, that young people must be respected, and, despite their all-knowing attitude and their virtual fearlessness, we must excuse them on the grounds of inexperience, in the knowledge that life will knock the corners off them and validate them as experiential and reflective learners.

I respect those whose lives are a witness to higher things. Their example gives us faith in ourselves and our abilities, giving us courage in faith, challenge, and hope that things can be better.

I believe that difference can add colour and richness to a discussion, to an ideal, and even to a culture, if meant with an informed regard.

Children must be valued at all times – their trust, their stories, their spontaneity; fragility's unquenchable reliance must be cherished – to revisit this worn-out world through new eyes and to re-invent seasons, symbols, the significance of people's own story, and the sacramentality of everyday things.'

Feeding time... Joe with his children Katie and Eoin on the banks of the Corrib River in Galway City

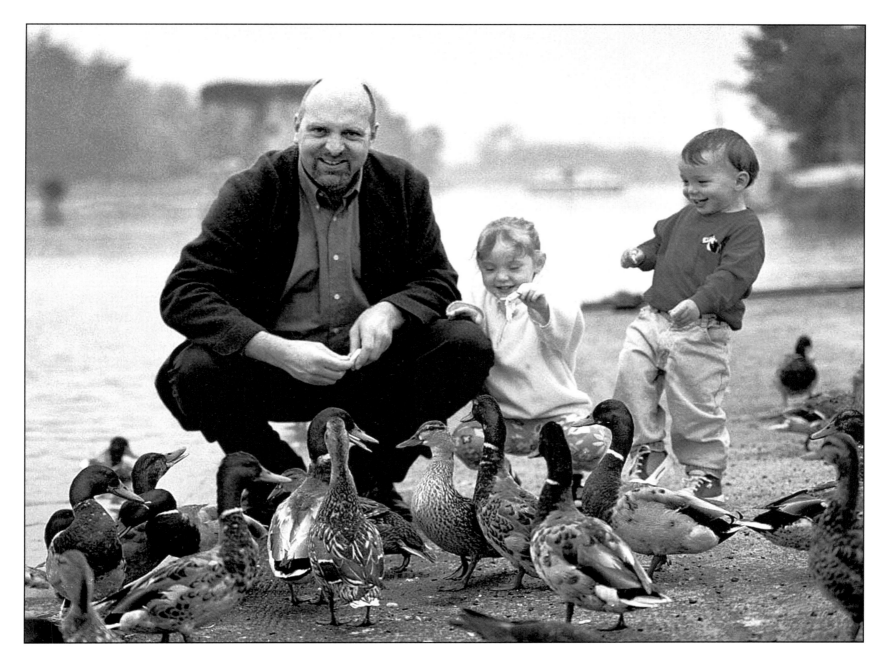

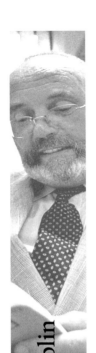

Dublin

David Norris

David Norris has been an Independent Senator in Dáil Éireann since 1987. He was a senior lecturer in the English Department in Trinity College, Dublin, from 1968–98. Educated at St Andrew's College, The High School, Reade Pianoforte School, and Trinity College, Dublin, David is a passionate advocate of human rights. He was principally responsible for the passing of the act decriminalising homosexual acts between consenting adults. He has fought successfully on behalf of the travelling community, the disabled, and refugees. Internationally, through successful lobbying and questioning of authorities in East Timor, and Tehran, he has challenged and heightened world awareness on the violation of human rights and treatment of minorities in those countries. David Norris is an authority on James Joyce, is chairman of the James Joyce Cultural Centre, and a regular broadcaster and world lecturer on the subject. He is chairman of North Great George's Street Preservation Society, a life member of Friends of St Patrick's Cathedral, and an honorary member of both the University Philisophical Society and the College Historical Society.

Work makes the man
The want of it the fellow
The rest's but leather and Prunella

'I found this in an occasional book of my grandfather's, written in his own handwriting. My aunt told me that she often remembered him quoting it. It means that real human values rather than social standing or affectation mark out the good human being.'

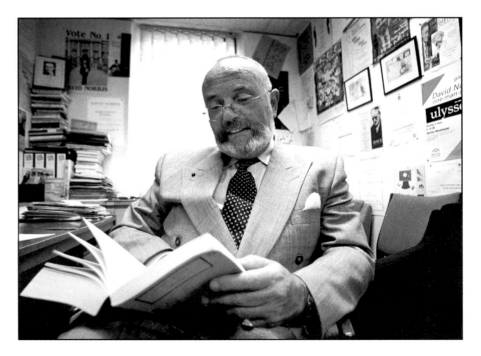

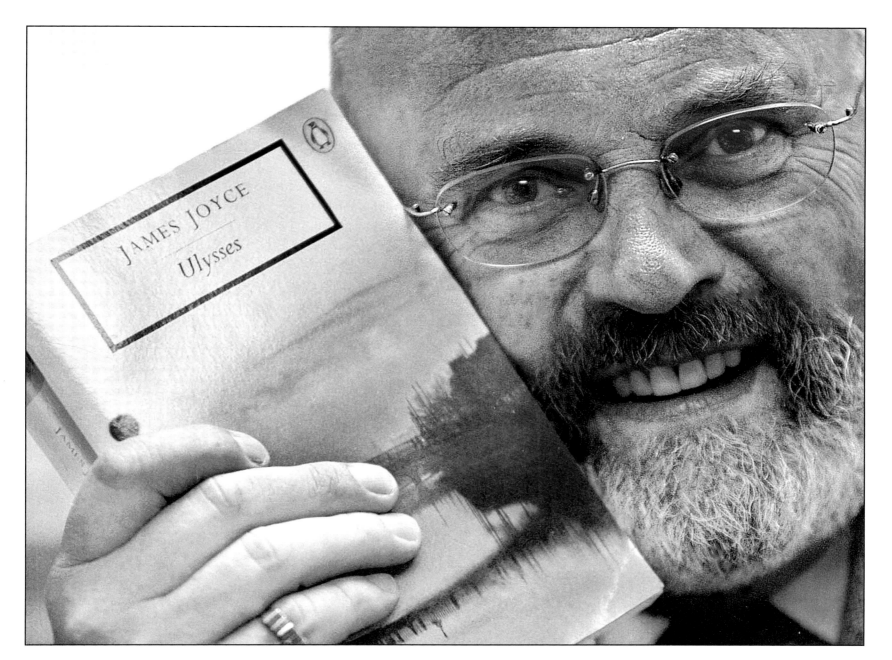

Andrew Redmond is a baritone who has recently graduated from the Royal Irish Academy of Music in Dublin. He is continuing his study at the Academy with Dr Veronica Dunne and *répétiteur* Dearbhla Collins. Andrew has won numerous competitions, including the Joseph O'Mara Cup for Male Operatic Aria at the Feis Ceoil in Dublin. As a concert soloist, he has worked with many of the country's leading choirs and choral societies, performing such works as Handel's Messiah, Bach's St Matthew Passion, Fauré's Requiem and Mozart's Requiem. Andrew is originally from Newbridge, County Kildare, and is the son of Elizabeth and the late Peter Redmond. He has three brothers, Simon, Paul and Timothy and enjoys reading and socialising!

Kildare

Andrew Redmond

And an old priest said, Speak to us of Religion.

And he said:

Have I spoken this day of aught else?

Is not religion all deeds and all reflection,

And that which is neither deed nor reflection, but a wonder and a surprise ever springing in the soul, even while the hands hew the stone or tend the loom?

Who can separate his faith from his actions, or his belief from his occupations?

Who can spread his hours before him, saying, 'This for God and this for myself; This for my soul and this other for my body'?

All your hours are wings that beat through space from self to self.

He who wears his morality but as his best garment were better naked.

The wind and the sun will tear no holes in his skin.

And he who defines his conduct by ethics imprisons his song-bird in a cage.

The freest song comes not through bars and wires.

And he to whom worshipping is a window, to open but also to shut, has not yet visited the house of his soul whose windows are from dawn to dawn.

Your daily life is your temple and your religion.

Whenever you enter into it take with you your all.

Take the plough and the forge and the mallet and the lute,

The things you have fashioned in necessity or for delight

For in reverie you cannot rise above your achievements nor fall lower than your failures.

And take with you all men:

For in adoration you cannot fly higher than their hopes nor humble yourself lower than their despair.

And if you would know God, be not therefore a solver of riddles.

Rather look about you and you shall see Him playing with your children.

And look into space; you shall see Him walking in the cloud, outstretching His arms in the lightning and descending in rain.

You shall see Him smiling in flowers, then rising and waving His hands in trees.

from *The Prophet* by Kahlil Gibran (1883–1931)

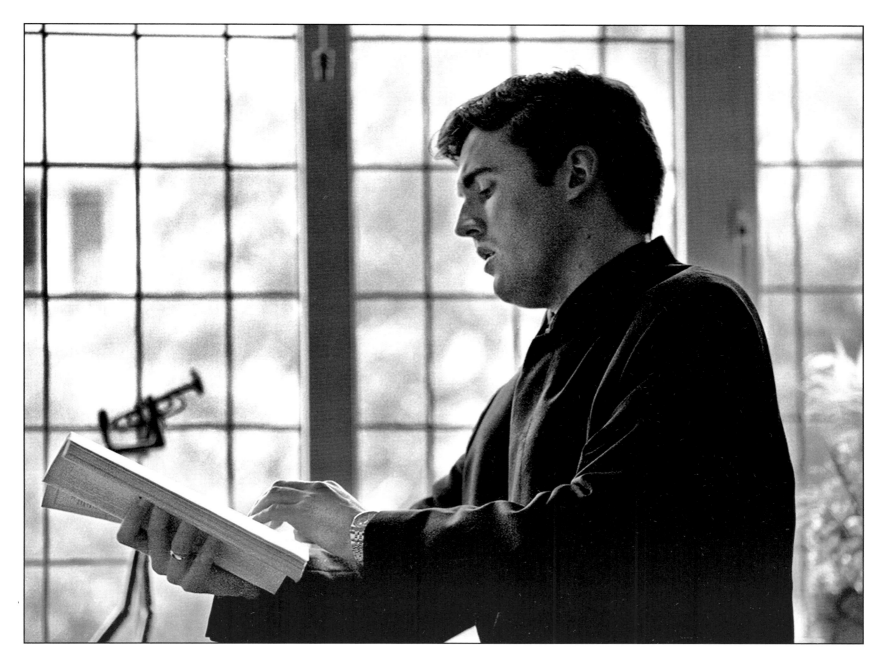

The Very Rev Robert MacCarthy is Dean of St Patrick's Cathedral in Dublin. He was elected by members of the Cathedral Chapter. Prior to his election he was Rector of St Nicholas's Collegiate Church and Provost of Tuam. Ordained in 1979, he was educated in St Columba's College, Rathfarnham, Dublin. He continued his studies in Trinity College, Dublin, St John's, Cambridge, Trinity College, Oxford, and Cuddesdon Theological College. He became curate of Carlow in 1979, and also held the position of Librarian of Pusey House, Oxford, and Fellow of St Cross College. In 1982, he was appointed Team Vicar in Bracknell New Town. Dean Robert was also Bishop's Vicar in Kilkenny Cathedral, and Rector of Castlecomer, County Kilkenny. His publications include *Ancient and Modern: A Short History of the Church of Ireland* and *The Trinity College Estates, 1800–1923: Corporate Management in an Age of Reform.* Robert enjoys architectural history as a pastime.

Dublin

Robert MacCarthy

Prayer of St Patrick (commonly called 'St Patrick's Breastplate')

I bind unto myself today the strong Name of the Trinity,
by invocation of the same, the three in one and one in three.

I bind this day to me forever, by pow'r of faith, Christ's incarnation;
His baptism in Jordan river; his death on cross for my salvation;
His bursting from the spiced tomb; his riding up the heav'nly way;
His coming at the day of doom; I bind unto myself today.

I bind unto myself the power of the great love of cherubim;
The sweet 'Well done' in judgement hour, the service of the seraphim,
Confessors' faith, apostles' word, the patriarchs' prayer, the prophets's scrolls,
All good deeds done unto the Lord, and purity of virgins souls.

I bind unto myself today the virtues of the star-lit heaven,
The glorious sun's life-giving ray, the whiteness of the moon at even,
The flashing of the lightning free, the whirling wind's tempestuous shocks,
The stable earth, the deep salt sea around the old eternal rocks.

I bind unto myself today the pow'r of God to hold, and lead,
His eye to watch, his might to say, his ear to hearken to my need;
The wisdom of my God to teach, his hand to guide me, his shield to ward;
The word of God to give me speech, his heavenly host to my guard:

Against the demon snares of sin, the vice that gives temptation force,
The natural lusts that war within, the hostile men that mar my course,
Or few or many, far or nigh, in every place, and in all hours,
Against their fierce hostility, I bind to me these holy powers.

Against all Satan's spells and wiles, against false words of heresy,
Against knowledge that defiles, against the heart's idolatry
Against the wizard's evil craft, against the death-wound and the burning,
The choking wave, the poisoned shaft, protect me, Christ, till my returning.

Christ be with me, Christ within me, Christ behind me, Christ before me,
Christ beside me, Christ to win me, Christ to comfort and restore me,
Christ beneath me, Christ above me, Christ in quiet, Christ in danger,
Christ in the hearts of all that love me, Christ in the mouth of friend and stranger.

I bind unto myself today the strong Name of the Trinity,
by invocation of the same, the three in one and one in three.
Of whom all nature hath creation; eternal Father, Spirit, Word;
Praise to the Lord of my salvation, salvation is of Christ the Lord.
Amen.

'Have you ever, I wonder, pondered the words of what is called "St Patrick's Breastplate" – if you have, I think you must have wondered at the astonishing radicalism of its conception of God. We stand at the end of a tradition of theology that so emphasised the transcendence of God as almost to exclude him from our world altogether – and certainly to exclude him from the world of nature. "The Breastplate" stands at the opposite end of the spectrum and emphasises the immanence of God – in our hearts, in the hearts of those we met, and it also points to the presence of God outside the human condition, in the world of nature. How seldom do we think of the glory of God as reflected by the star-lit heaven; by the glorious sun's life-giving ray; by the witness of the moon at evening; by the flashing of lightning; or to be seen in the whirling winds tempestuous shocks? And we live our lives without acknowledging that Christ is a contemporary reality in our world: in quiet, in danger, in hearts of all that love us – mouth of friend and stranger.'

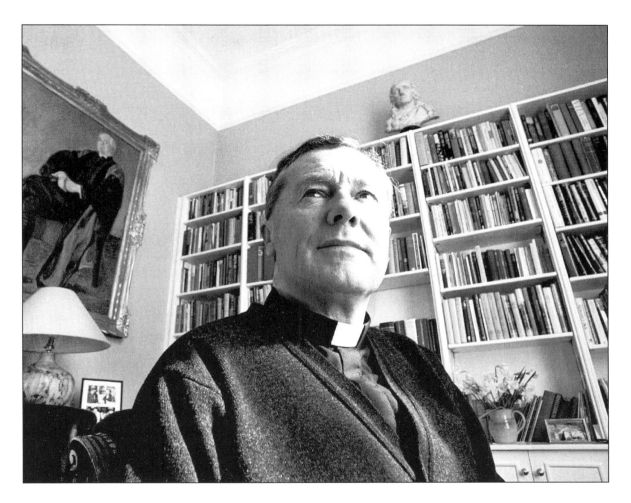

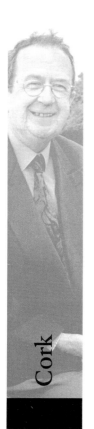

Declan Hassett is Arts Editor of *The Irish Examiner*. An award-winning theatre critic, he was editor of the *Evening Echo* from 1976 to 1985, having become a staff journalist in 1962. He has lived all his life in Blackrock, Cork. Declan is married to Anne (née O'Connell) and they have eight children, Ita, Declan, Clodagh, Michael, Áine, Niamh, David and Brian. They also had a daughter Orla who died aged ten months and who was the subject of the first chapter ('Unshed Tears') of his book *The Way We Were*. Declan is also the author of the best-selling *All Our Yesterdays*, and his play *Rebels* was premiered at the Everyman Palace, Cork. Declan enjoys walking in Ardmore and golfing in Lismore, County Waterford.

Cork

Declan Hassett

A Sense of Place

'I grew up with a pervasive sense of place. There has never been a time in my life when I did not thank God for the joy of growing up in Blackrock, two miles from Cork city, surrounded on three sides by the Lee, Lough Mahon and the Douglas Estuary.... Blackrock, Ballinlough, Ballinsheen, Beaumont, Ballintemple, and Ballinure were our rural retreats on the edge of the city not yet bloated, nor too full of its own importance.... From market gardens to walled estates, wild meadows to stony shores, salmon boats at anchor by Marina's end, as the first of the Innisfallens took lonely sons and daughters of the south to foggy London town. Parents prayed by Penrose Quay that their darlings would write and be all right in a world of which they knew little.... Fox and hare swept over open fields, the rabbit, weasel, badger and hare had the place to themselves until we, the only known tribe of short pants Comanches, went on the war-path down by the woods and searched for pale-faces from across the Black Bridge that was always painted red.... Summer arrived and they'd cut the first hay, toss it, turn it, let it lie in the sun before it would be racked, placed in cocks as bees would rise, disturbed, wishing we would buzz off as we'd search for the corncrake or check ivy-covered walls for birds eggs when there was no one looking.

By stone walls we kissed our first kisses and wondered what was all the fuss about when we could be spending our precious time fishing for tadpoles in the little pond in the wood but making sure we'd be home for a night tea of 'blacka' jam and our mothers' rocky buns. The wild flowers and hedgerows, the boithrins and woodlands, the precious places of our carefree days have gone and there is little enough to remind us of the way we were...'

Declan Hassett with Blackrock Castle by Lough Mahon's shore in the background

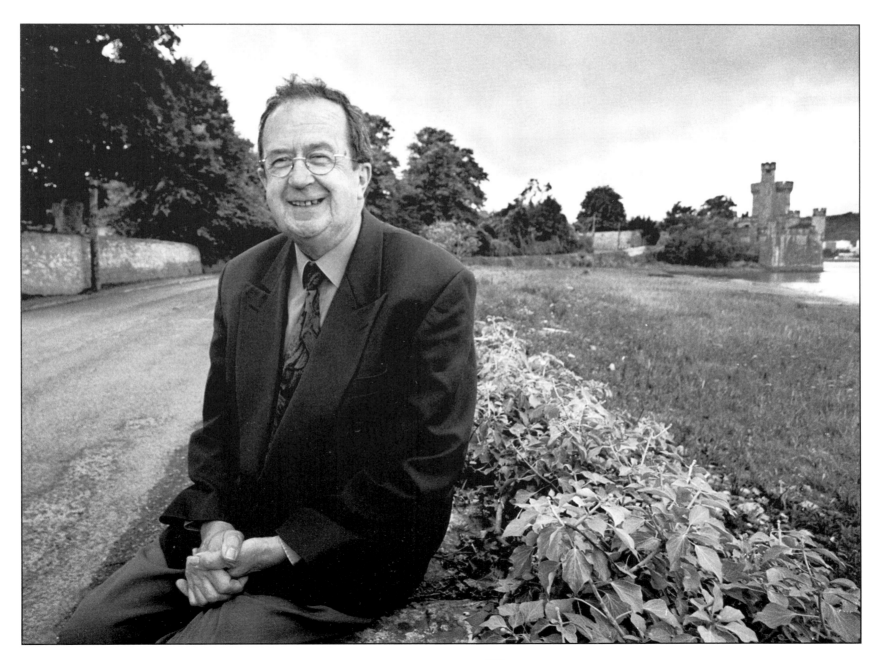

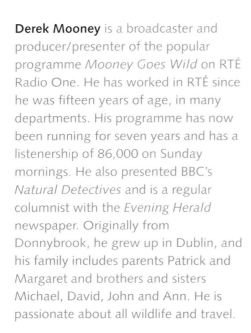

Derek Mooney

Dublin

Derek Mooney is a broadcaster and producer/presenter of the popular programme *Mooney Goes Wild* on RTÉ Radio One. He has worked in RTÉ since he was fifteen years of age, in many departments. His programme has now been running for seven years and has a listenership of 86,000 on Sunday mornings. He also presented BBC's *Natural Detectives* and is a regular columnist with the *Evening Herald* newspaper. Originally from Donnybrook, he grew up in Dublin, and his family includes parents Patrick and Margaret and brothers and sisters Michael, David, John and Ann. He is passionate about all wildlife and travel.

'In 1992, I went on a whale-watching trip to Baja California in Mexico. Each year Gray whales migrate there from the frigid environs of the Chukchi and Bering seas. They come to breed in the warm waters of the Pacific lagoons. It's quite an incredible journey, some 5,000 miles, and it's witnessed by thousands of enthusiastic whale watchers all along the western seaboard of the United States of America.

The final destination for the whales is the Laguna San Ignacio and it was there that I had my first encounter with these gentle giants. It was an amazing experience just to sit in a small fishing boat and observe these magnificent creatures. I remember on one occasion a forty-foot long Gray whale came towards us and gently nudged the boat away from her newborn calf.

Today, whale-watching is a huge tourist industry worth billions of dollars, and to think it's not all that long ago that we lived in a harpoon economy.'

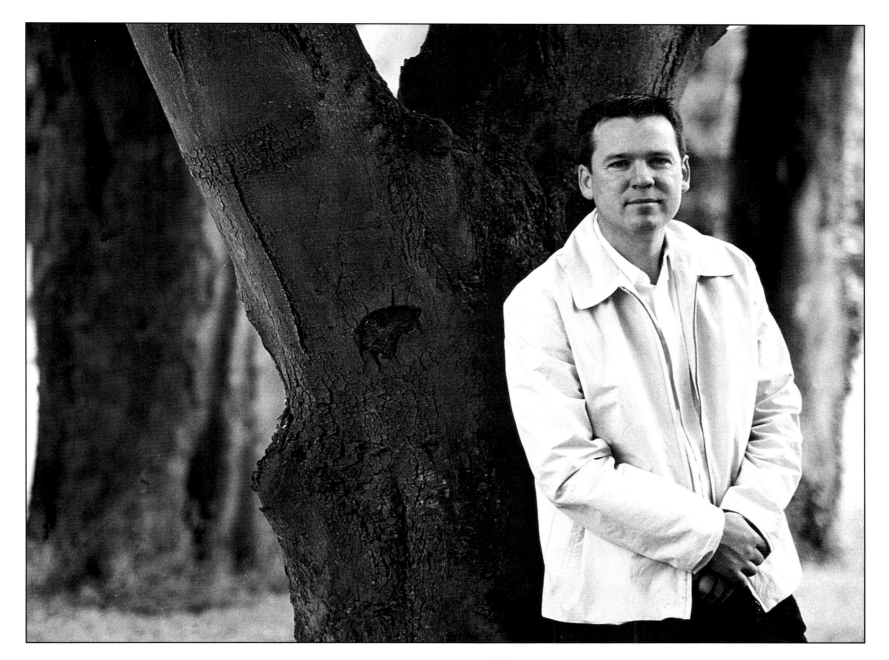

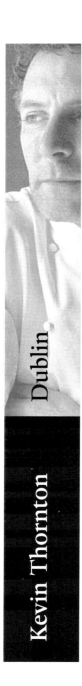

Dublin

Kevin Thornton

Kevin Thornton is chef and proprietor of Thornton's Restaurant on Portobello Road in Dublin City. He runs the restaurant with his wife Muriel O'Connor. Originally from Cashel, County Tipperary, after graduating from Galway RTC, Kevin travelled to London to work in Walton's, then Switerland and Canada before returning to work at the Shelbourne Hotel. He also worked at the Michelin-starred restaraunt of Paul Bocuse in Lyons, and taught at the College of Catering in Cathal Brugha Street, Dublin.The philosophy of his cooking is to be true to the fine produce, to treat it with respect, and coax out the flavours to create dishes that he can be proud of. Kevin's menu is a testimony to this passionate philosophy of food and nature. Dishes include roast squab, pigeon, truffles, rabbit, crawfish, scallops and pig's trotter. He has won many awards, including Chef of the Year 1996, Gilbey's gold medal 1996, a star from the Egon Ronay Guide 96/97, and a rosette from the Michelin Guide 96/97. Kevin and Muriel have two sons, Conor and Edward. Kevin enjoys photography, wild food, mountain walks, scuba-diving and swimming.

'I'm privileged to be doing what I do. In the kitchen we work as a team using natural energy. It is in my cooking that I find my spirituality. All life has a soul. Take the tomato: it is planted in the ground, nurtured, feeding from the sun and the rain; it is perfect. I must look after it to ensure it looks perfect on the plate. The beauty of the shrimp – the most beautiful fish in the world – and I must put my influence on it… having a respect for life in all forms. This privilege must not be abused. When you get your produce, only then can you decide on the dish; we work in reverse! We must look after the food to the best of our ability, bringing it to a different dimension, utilising our energy, like a chain reaction in the kitchen. It is so important to understand the produce – sourcing fish from west Cork, lamb from Wicklow and pig from Monaghan – using as much Irish as possible. What I strive for is perfection and that, of course, is never reached; you can never do the same dish twice. You have to criticise yourself all the time to be better… try to reach new levels all the time… spiritual levels… that's my way of communicating. It's my life.'

Lovers drink wine all day and night
and tear the veils of the mind.
When drunk with love's wine
body, heart and soul
become one.

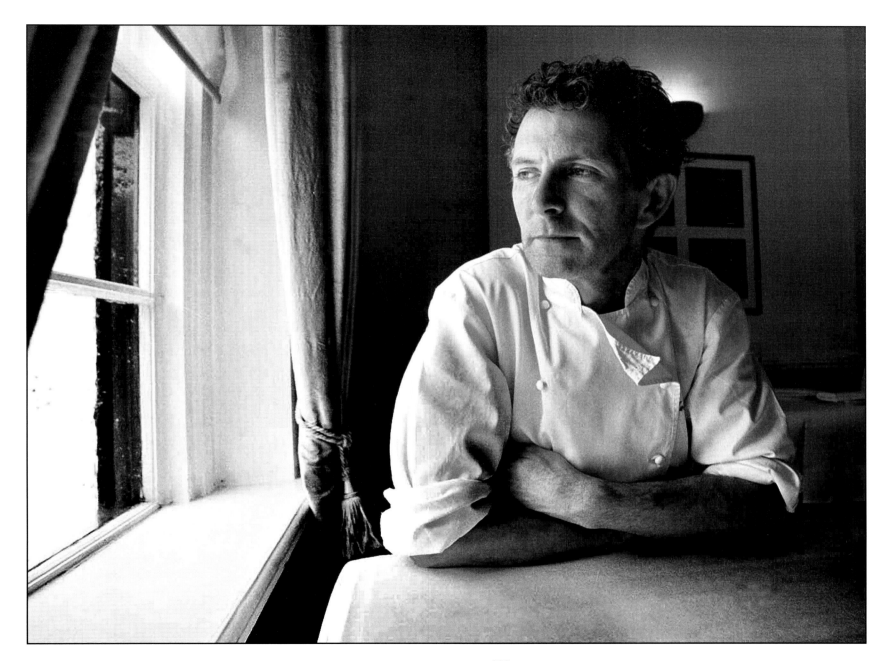

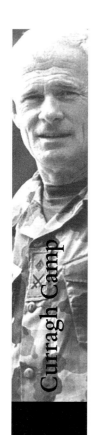

Curragh Camp

Colm Doylen

Lieutenant Colonel Colm Doyle is School Comdt of the United Nations Training School at the Military College, Curragh Camp. He joined the army in 1964 and was commissioned in 1966. He has held many commands, serving in Cyprus in 1968, in Lebanon as UN Military Observer from 1984 to 1986, and with the European Community Monitor Mission (ECMM). Colm was personal representative to Lord Carrington, the Chairman of the International Peace Conference in Yugoslavia, and was involved in ceasefire and hostage deals with all sides of the dispute. In 1997, he commanded the Irish Battalion in Lebanon and served as director of public relations in the Defence Force. Originally from Ardee, County Louth, Colm is married to Gráinne and they have four children, Elaine, Mark, Sheena and Shane. Now living in Limerick, his interests include current affairs, DIY and sport.

'My perception of a refugee had been of somebody from a far-away country, say the "Third World", remote, poor, and seemingly unimportant. Then I experienced Bosnia, where I met refugees wearing fur coats, well-educated and with professional qualifications, all struggling through the snow of Sarajevo with nowhere to go, lost and terrified. This was the reality of ethnic cleansing, and it was being carried out in the heart of Europe.'

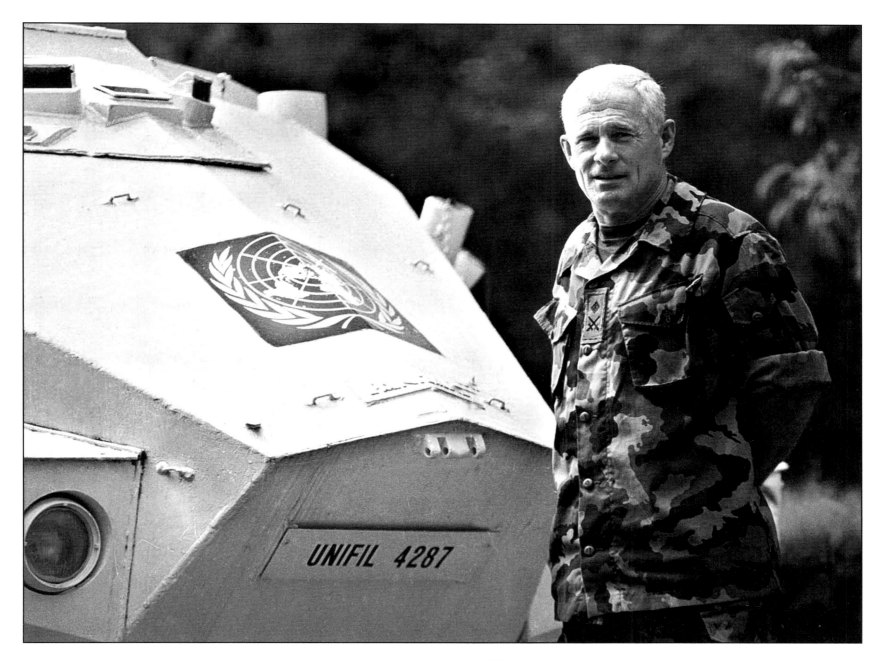

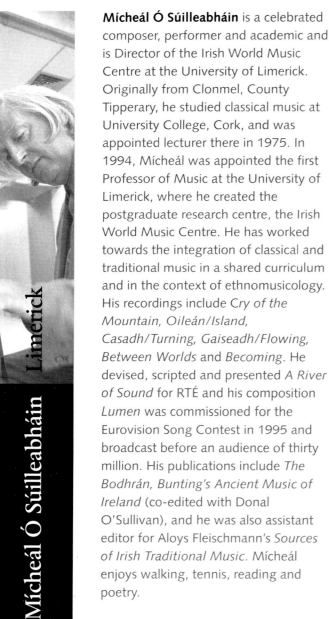

Limerick

Mícheál Ó Súilleabháin

Mícheál Ó Súilleabháin is a celebrated composer, performer and academic and is Director of the Irish World Music Centre at the University of Limerick. Originally from Clonmel, County Tipperary, he studied classical music at University College, Cork, and was appointed lecturer there in 1975. In 1994, Mícheál was appointed the first Professor of Music at the University of Limerick, where he created the postgraduate research centre, the Irish World Music Centre. He has worked towards the integration of classical and traditional music in a shared curriculum and in the context of ethnomusicology. His recordings include *Cry of the Mountain, Oileán/Island, Casadh/Turning, Gaiseadh/Flowing, Between Worlds* and *Becoming*. He devised, scripted and presented *A River of Sound* for RTÉ and his composition *Lumen* was commissioned for the Eurovision Song Contest in 1995 and broadcast before an audience of thirty million. His publications include *The Bodhrán, Bunting's Ancient Music of Ireland* (co-edited with Donal O'Sullivan), and he was also assistant editor for Aloys Fleischmann's *Sources of Irish Traditional Music*. Mícheál enjoys walking, tennis, reading and poetry.

Templum

The sea is a temple.
Vested in seaweed.
Priestly fish find coral waters.
Undercurrents beat time.
Overhead, where light and waters meet,
Blind ships take soundings.
My temples are riverbanks for the templum of the sea.
Poor Pilot,
I stand at the crown of my sacred vessel
Trusting the North star,
Journeying home.

'I wrote this poem in 1993 during the transition period when I was finishing up my work at University College, Cork, and moving to the University of Limerick where I was to set up the Irish World Music Centre. I was also right in the middle of writing the score for the 1925 silent movie entitled *Irish Destiny*. The poem became the inspiration for the opening meditation music of the mass *Missa Gadelica*, which I wrote in 1994. I think the poem is about subsonic listening in order to attempt to pick up soundings that will guide us home. The undercurrents of the sea beat time to a different rhythm to the tempos of the world we live in. The third eye exists towards the crown of the head whose temples are like riverbanks containing deep secrets of the temple of the sea. The gravity of the north star is our reference point towards a new building.'

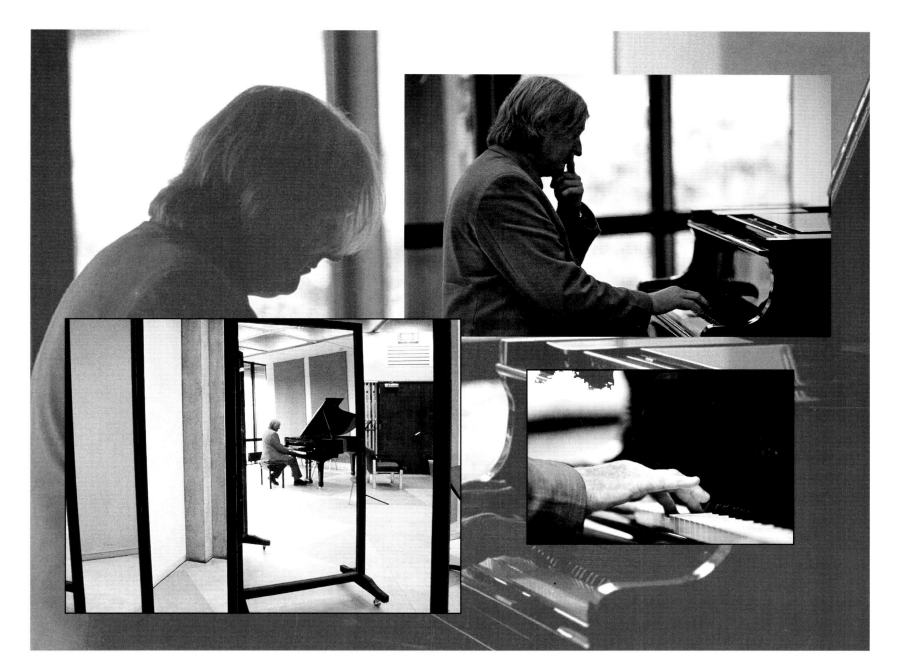

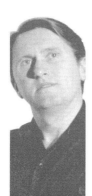

Tralee

Oliver Hurley

Oliver Hurley is Artistic Director of Siamsa Tíre, The National Folk Theatre of Ireland based in Tralee, County Kerry. He joined Siamsa Tíre at just nine years of age and became one of the core full-time members on leaving school. Prior to Oliver's appointment as Artistic Director, he was Associate Director with its founder Fr Pat Ahern, and was also dance captain of the group. He has produced many of the group's shows, including *Samhain*, *Crann Sí*, and *Oisín*. Oliver is orignally from Tralee and is married to Geraldine who is a performer with the company. They have three children, Clíona, Níamh and Darragh. In his spare time Oliver directs and choreographs with musical societies around the country. He won best director/choreographer for *The Mikado* with the Tralee Musical Society. Any other spare time is spent with his wife and three lively children!

'My involvement in church music introduced me to a beautiful prayer, set to music by Fr Pat Ahern a few years ago. The prayer originated from the lips of an old woman in the west Kerry Gaeltacht. When the local priest would pay a visit to her, she would recite this prayer on receiving Holy Communion from him. Her humility is a gentle reminder to us all in this time of prosperity.'

A Íosa mhilis. A Íosa mhilis. A Íosa mhilis.
Ní suíocháin duit mo theanga, ní lóistín duit mo chroí.
Ach bronn orm do bheannaitheacht is go bhfána – sé 'gam choíche.
A Íosa mhilis. A Íosa mhilis. A Íosa mhilis.
Ní suíocháin duit mo theanga, ní lóistín duit mo chroí.
Ach bronn orm do bheannaitheacht is go bhfána – sé 'gam choíche.

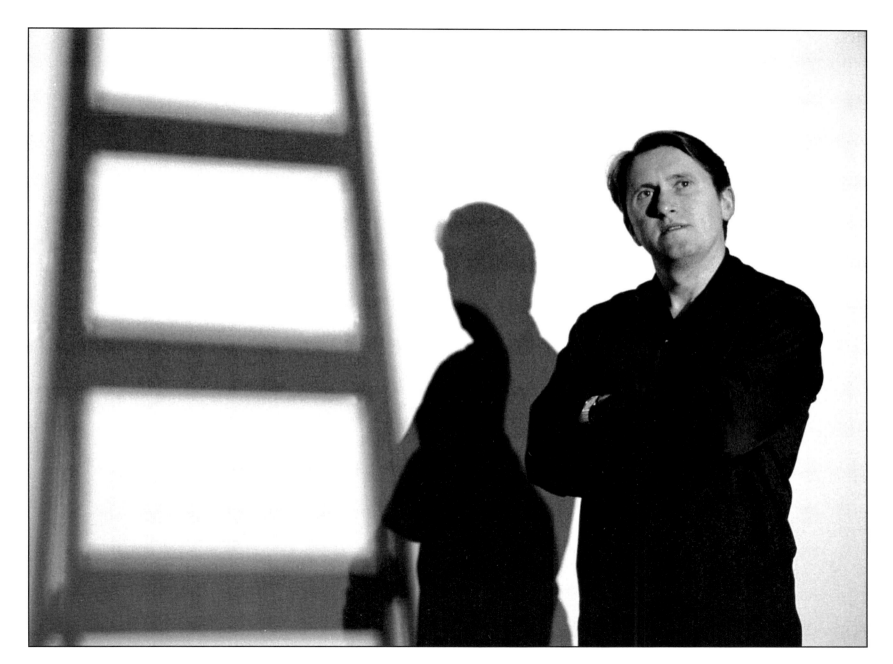

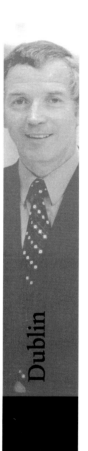

Dublin

John Lonergan

John Lonergan is Governor of Mountjoy Prison, Dublin. He has worked in the prison service since 1968 and became Governor in 1984. His unique and individual style is well documented. He is responsible for the management of both the men and women's prison, which have a staff of 600 and 700 prisoners respectively. Meeting the individual needs of the prisoner is a priority in Mountjoy. John has instilled this basic need since his appointment. He is a native of Tipperary, is married to Breda, and they have two daughters, Sinéad and Máire. John is on the board of management of the Pro-Cathedral and they run a drop-in agency and day-care centre. He is also involved with Ruhama – an agency to assist women on the run. John enjoys running, all sports, especially hurling, and is involved with Kilmacud Crokes in Dublin. His other interests include current affairs, drama and reading.

'Meeting the individual needs of the prisoner is a big responsibility within this system, making sure that the prisoner is heard and that they receive and perceive justice in prison. The most important thing is that their voice is heard. There are injustices built into the system. We must all remember that each prisoner is an individual.

Issuing a presence of humanity is important – I have to demonstrate that humanity. It is often so popular to be inhuman within a prison. After all, they are sent here to be punished. The easy way out for me is not to insist on humane practices. Life is all about living the Gospel rather than reading it or quoting from the Bible. I try to live the Gospel with my interaction and relationship with the prisoners. They are at the last line of hope when they arrive to us.

We have to demonstrate an atmosphere of justice, and justice is linked to listening to "the enemy". For me, the enemy deserves to be heard. It gives you a completely different perspective. Every human being has a story to tell and the challenge is, as an individual, to hear that story.'

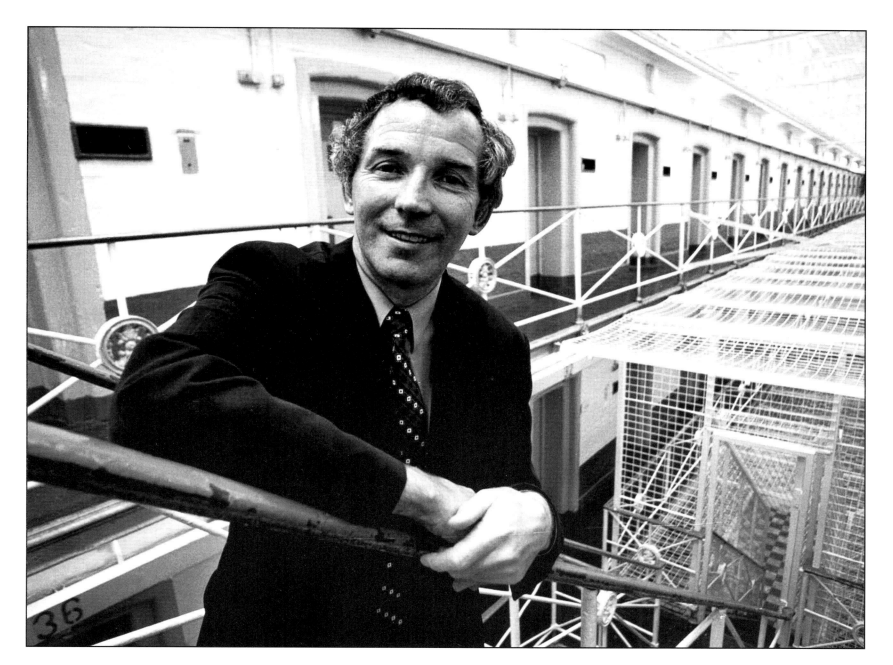

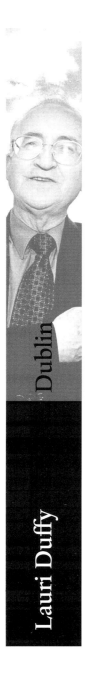

Dublin

Lauri Duffy

Lauri Duffy is a travel agent who specialises in tours to Fatima in Portugal. He brings at least two groups of pilgrims each week, from May to October. For him and his wife Veronica it is a labour of love. They conduct the tours personally, giving the pilgrims a deep insight into the message of Fatima. Prior to setting up the travel agency, Lauri worked with CIÉ and Guinness. Lauri is a specialist in transport and is a fellow of the Chartered Institute of Transport. He is former chairman of the prestigious Transport Policy Committee of the Confederation of Irish Industry. Married to Veronica Daly from Lahinch, they have two children, Marie-Therese and Joseph. Lauri's main hobby is making videos. He has scripted and co-produced videos of Fatima that have been distributed widely in many languages.

'My earliest memory of an event was being brought by my mother to a convent and being placed on my knees before a lighted candle and a statue of Our Lady. I was being "dedicated" to Our Lady. Perhaps the reason this event stuck in my memory so clearly is that my older brothers taunted me if I did anything not pleasing to them with the sarcasm: "That's a nice way to behave for a boy who has been dedicated to Our Lady!"

It was a Christian Brother who prepared me for my First Holy Communion. Br O'Driscoll instilled in me a special love for Our Lady and taught me prayers that concluded with: "I ask this grace through the merits of Mary my Holy Mother". He picked the 8th of December, the Feast of the Immaculate Conception, for my First Communion

My first job was in CIÉ. I was pleasantly surprised to discover that one of the perks was free railway travel throughout Europe. This I used to visit famous shrines of Our Lady. My first visit to Fatima was in 1954. There I met a priest from Goa, Fr Mascarenhas. He showed me everything – I even met the parents of Blessed Francisco and Blessed Jacinta. I went home enthralled with Fatima, so much so that I returned there the following year, despite the fact that the rail journey took three days in each direction!

I took early retirement in 1988 and started to bring people to Fatima. Although I have had many interesting jobs, I have never before had anything like the "job satisfaction" of showing groups of people around Fatima and knowing that many of them are drawn closer to our Heavenly Mother.

Was finding this work a bit of good luck? Or was it Br O'Driscoll? Or Fr Mascarenhas? Or was it my mother – which of them?!'

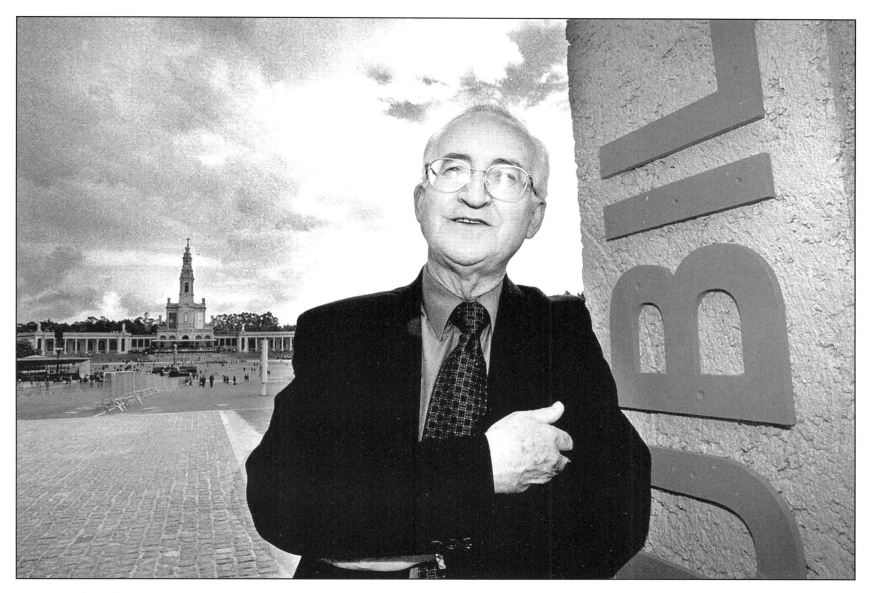

Lauri stands in the main Basilica square in Fatima after the beatification of Blessed Jacinta and Blessed Francisco Marto by Pope John Paul II in May 2000

Malachí Quinn is an account manager at Slattery PR, based in Merrion Street, Dublin. He has worked there for three years. Malachí's job involves media relations, getting clients' names known on radio and television and into print. Malachí is responsible for Bank of Ireland, Carlsberg, Mount Juliet Golf Club, Toyota Ireland and IRFU. Prior to joining Slattery PR, he worked in sports management. Malachí was born in Athens, grew up in Sandymount, and now lives in Ringsend with his partner Erika Fagan. His family includes parents Nicola Underwood-Quinn and Ruairí Quinn, his sister Síne and brother Conan. His pastimes are current affairs, history, sport, and hillwalking in Connemara.

'I find the best time to meditate or reflect is when I am running. When running, the mind and body are one and thus the mind can be released. It is a difficult place to describe, but one where I have always found peace and tranquillity, where meditation and reflection come naturally. A reflection that I aspire to is by Kahlil Gibran from the book *The Prophet*: "You give but little when you give of your possessions. It is when you give of yourself that you truly give".'

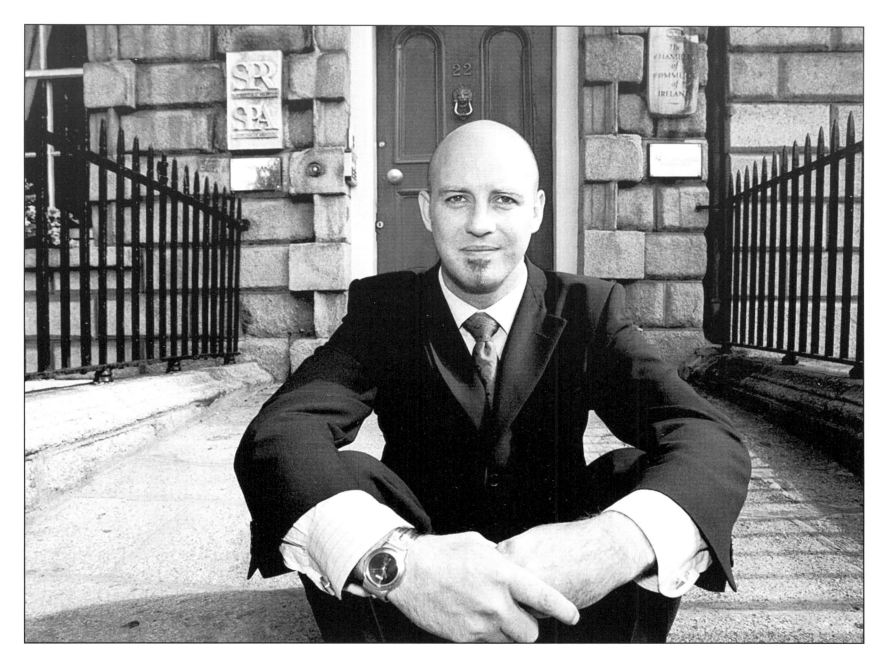

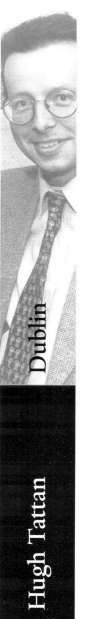

Dublin

Hugh Tattan

Hugh Tattan is the only child of renowned mezzo-soprano Bernadette Greevy and the late Peter Tattan. Born in Dublin, he was educated at Holy Faith Convent, Clontarf, and subsequently at St Paul's College, Clontarf. A talented animator, he worked with O'Sullivan Bluth Animation Studios in Dublin. Following their closure he worked with various smaller animation studios in Dublin, and as assistant manager of Chapters book store before moving to Stockholm, Sweden, where he now lives and works at Filmteckname animators. He is engaged to Linda Cammenberg from Skockholm.

The Angelus

The angel of the Lord declared unto Mary, and she was conceived by the Holy Ghost
(Hail Mary)
Behold the handmaid of the Lord. Be it done to me according to your word.
(Hail Mary)
And the word was made Flesh, and dwelt amongst us.
(Hail Mary)
Pray for us, O holy Mother of God, that we may be worthy of the promises of Christ. Pour forth we beseech you, O Lord, your grace into our hearts, that we to whom the incarnation of Christ our Lord was made known by a message of an angel, may by his passion and Cross be brought to the glory of His Resurrection, through Christ our Lord. May the divine assistance remain always with us, and may the souls of all the faithful departed, through the mercy of God, rest in peace. Amen.

'I have always loved the Angelus, and recite it whenever I can, even here in Sweden where the Angelus bell does not ring out. This beautiful prayer reminds us of the miracle of the incarnation and sums up in simple words the whole basis and heart of our faith.'

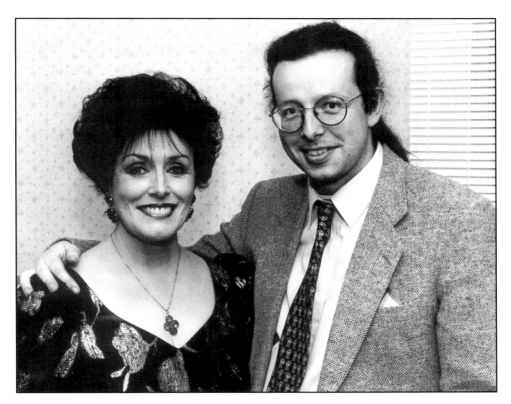

Hugh Tattan with his mother, mezzo soprano Bernadette Greavy
(photo from Bernadette's family collection).

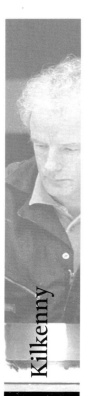

Francis Tansey

Francis Tansey is a full-time professional artist at Ballyreddin Art Studio, Bennett's Bridge, County Kilkenny, where he also resides. He is a graduate of the National College of Art and Design, Dublin. In 1985 he became the first artist in residence at the Butler Art Gallery, County Kilkenny. Francis specialises in geometric colour field painting using acrylic on canvas. He has exhibited in galleries in California, Los Angeles, Malibu, Dublin, London, Brussels, France, Germany and, of course, Kilkenny. His many collections include commissions for Jefferson Smurfit Group plc, the National Concert Hall, Aer Rianta, The Arts Council of Ireland, Autobahn Music and the Ulster Museum. Francis is originally from Dundrum from a well-known cycling family – his father Joe Daly is the famous cycle dealer in Dublin and his brother is cyclist Paul Tansey. Other family members include Kathleen, David, Bernadette (Francis's twin), Catherine and Claire. Francis enjoys cycling, swimming, walking, music, gardening, and the company of his two cats, Yoda and Alice.

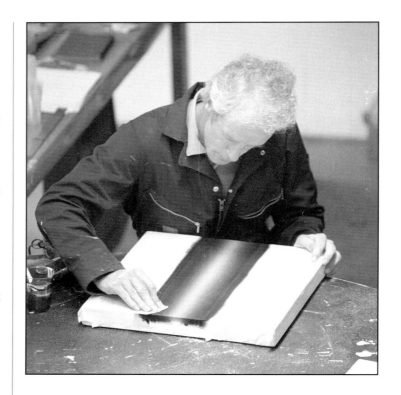

'The medium I have chosen is acrylic on canvas. The technique I use is one I have been using and developing for twenty years, that is, using rollers to apply repeated thin transparent layers of blended colours until the desired luminosity is achieved.

My work is primarily concerned with colour and its spatial dimensions. First I fill the background space with colour and then use geometry to create a universal language.'

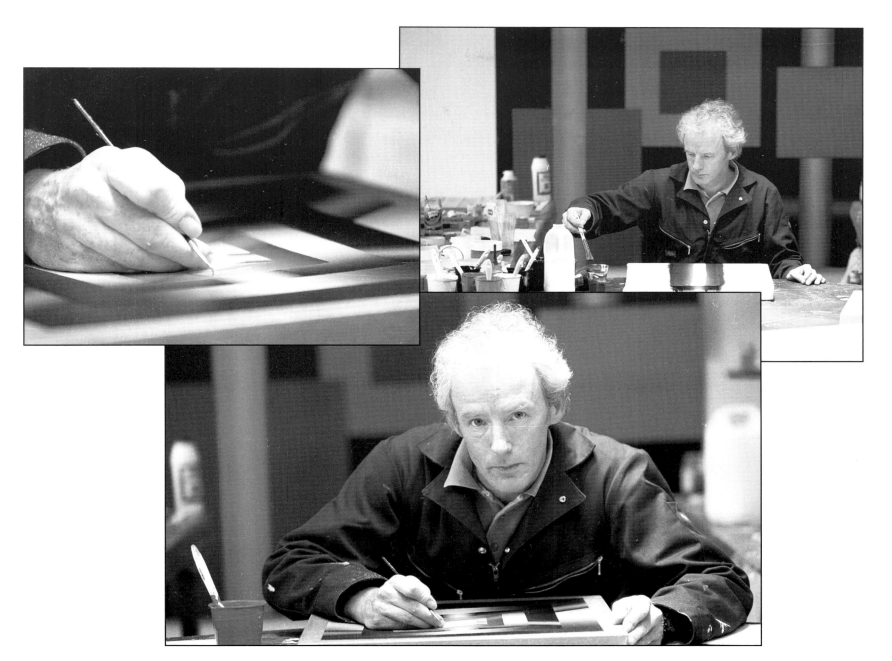

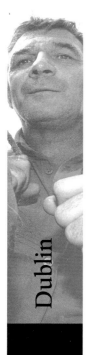

Mickey O'Neill

Mickey O'Neill is a horse trader based in Dublin. His family have been in the trade for over three hundred years. Mickey sells his stock in Ireland, England, Naples and France. He is Chairman of The Dublin Horse Association and Director of Smithfield Horse Fair and the Horse Owners Association. Mickey successfully negotiated with Dublin Corporation for the re-opening of The Smithfield Fair in Dublin city centre. He is at the heart of the Ballyfermot Partnership where they are building an equestrian centre and a training programme to teach and educate the young community to train, groom and look after the welfare of their horses. He set up the Ballyfermot Pony Club in 1972 and they race in Finglas every Sunday. Mickey was born in the Liberties and reared in Ballyfermot. He is married to Rose and they have two children, Ryan and Sandra, and one grandchild, Christopher. Horses are his life.

'Horses...how can I express my love for horses? When I sell a horse the adrenaline is flowing. I go straight out and buy another one.

Life wasn't always like this. When I was young I experienced awful hardship. I had four brothers who all died of muscular dystrophy. I used to wash, dress and carry them around. I was the only one working bringing in a wage. My father was in prison and my mother couldn't do it all. I had two sisters as well. When I look back at this life and see the kids in the area today, they don't realise how lucky they are. I do my best with them, introducing them to the world of horses, teaching them how to look after them and showing them the trade. I try to keep them out of trouble. Working with photographer Perry Ogden on his book *Pony Kids* was great. It was a great success and fantastic for us.

A few years ago I suffered a brain haemorrhage. I fought my way back and now I'm just doing my best. I often think how lucky I really am. In those times there was no time for emotions, and we never heard of counselling. I wouldn't like to see anyone go through the hardship I did.'

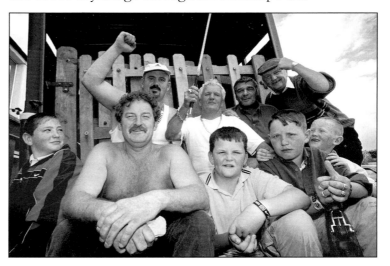

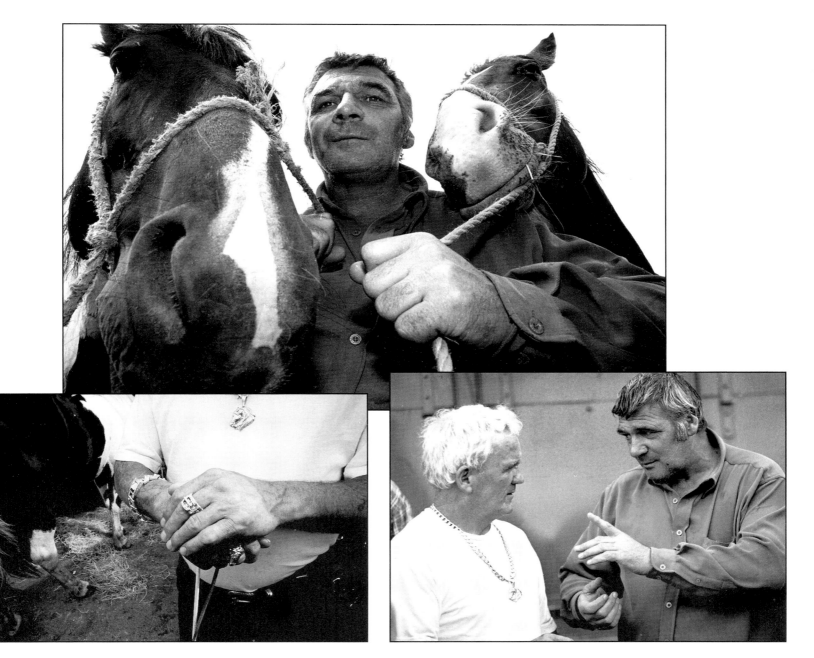

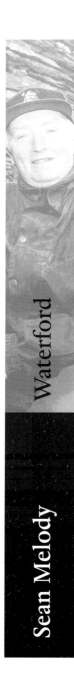

Sean Melody is a priest in the diocese of Waterford and Lismore. He has recently finished his term as Director of Veritas, a position held by him for the past seven years. Prior to that he worked in religious education and served as religious education advisor to the diocese. Sean is a native of Ballymacarbery, Clonmel, which is situated in the Nire Valley. He studied for the priesthood at Maynooth College from 1964 to 1972. Sean has two brothers, David and Pat, and one sister, Maura. He enjoys music, golfing and has a keen interest in hurling and soccer.

'Presence is a wonderful gift. We value the presence of friends and loved ones. God is ever present to us in so many varied ways, yet we seem at times to miss or not realise that God is in our presence as well as our being in God's presence.

Recently I celebrated baptism with a family in Waterford. I watched little John nestled in his mother's arms against her breasts and thought what a wonderful image of our presence to God and God's presence to us. No words were needed to express this closeness of mother and child; nor are words needed, very often, to express our closeness to God – just being present is all that matters.

In some of the "lesser moments", we can be helped by words, and there are many wonderful expressions created by others that we can draw upon. For this collection, I choose a reflection from *The Calm Beneath the Storm,* as an expression of what God's presence in us, and our presence in God, might mean.'

To Do What is Good in My Life

Lord, I really want to do something good with my life.
I see the needs of the world I'm part of,
one million poor in my own country,
people killed each day through violence,
old people living lonely and in squalor,
kids of my own age drugging themselves as an escape from life.

I know there are needs,
There are people who cannot live
Without the dedicated help of your friends.

I hear your call,
Sometimes a whisper, other times a gentle shout,
Inviting me to your presence,
Through my own personality and my own talents,

And with all my weaknesses,
In the world of these people.
But, Lord, I'm afraid.
I don't know if I can do anything for them.
I don't know how you want me to follow you:
Married? Single? Religious? A Priest?
I'm not sure I can give without losing so much myself.

Faith is what I ask, and light and love:
Faith to believe in your risen power at the foot of your cross,
Light to know the way you're asking me to serve you,
And love to trust that it's all possible.

Donal Neary

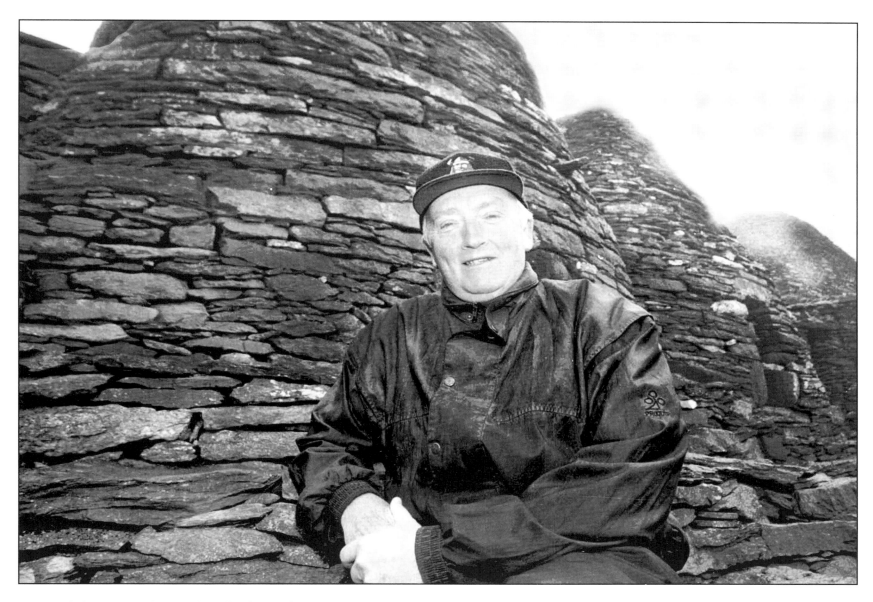

Sean Melody is pictured on Sceilig Mhicíl, one of the most westerly points in Europe, and one of the Skellig Islands, which lie eight miles off the Kerry coast. The hermitage, with its famous beehive dwellings, was occupied by the monks of Skellig in the sixth century.

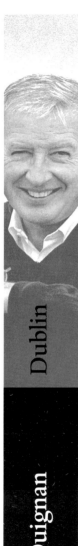

Sean Duignan

Sean Duignan is a presenter of *The Week in Politics* on RTÉ television. He joined RTÉ in 1964, was political correspondent for many years and anchor man on the *Six-One* news. Prior to joining RTÉ he was a reporter with *The Connaught Tribune* and *The Irish Independent* newspaper. He was Government Press Secretary for three years during the government of former Taoiseach Albert Reynolds. Sean is married to Marie (née Falvey) from Killorglin, and their family includes sons Mark and Neill, daughter Eileen and one grandchild Ciara. A Jacobs Award winner for broadcasting, Sean is author of the best-selling book *One Spin on the Merry-go-round*. He describes himself as 'an enthusiastic social drinker' and is millennium captain of the Dublin Journalists' Golfing Society.

'I come from the beautiful fishing village of Claddagh in Galway. My people came from Connemara where Irish was my first language. I had to learn to speak English when I went to school. That was the culture of Galway in the 1950s. My father was a Fianna Fáil TD and my mother died at the age of ninety five – only last year. My sister Roisín, who I'm very close to, lives in Galway.

A sense of place is so important. I often find that men drift towards their wife's background. For me it was Kerry where Marie is from. We're married for thirty five years. Even before that I was always fascinated with Kerry in a supplicated way, especially its people. I remember the Kerrymen coming to Galway University in the 1950s; they were so confident, especially the north Kerry lads. It was a combination of madness and brilliance; they were mad poets, mad drinkers and mad artists. I found that extraordinarily attractive. There was a certain distinctiveness about them. I often think there are so many places in Ireland that are more interesting than any part of the world and I want to see them all.

I look at my life in RTÉ and think, yes, there *is* such a diversity of cultures here, it is a very interesting village, not as soulless as the buildings look, every enthusiast catered for – traditional players, drama, business, politics, gardening – all walks of life. I love that aspect, it's what makes RTÉ so interesting.

When I wrote *One Spin on the Merry-go-round* I always believed that we really only get one spin, so let's seize the day! I realised the truth in that sentiment when I was very ill a few years ago. Now that I'm well, I want to enjoy every bit of it. We really only have one good shot at life. I love that theory about the fellow with the custard pie waiting around the corner to slap you in the face. Go and enjoy life before the man with the custard pie hits you.'

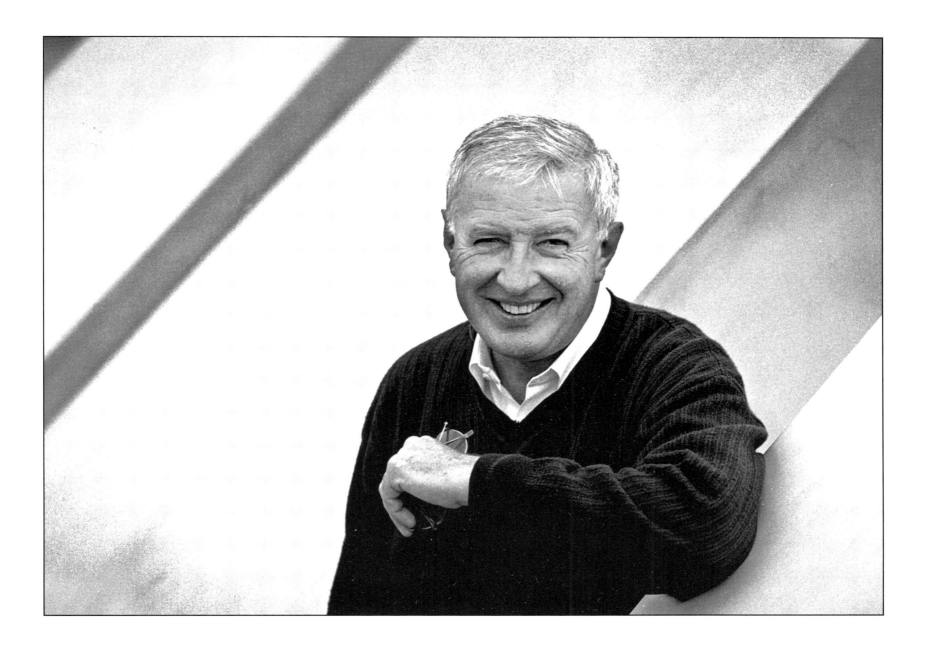

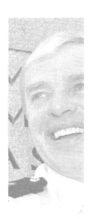

Dublin

John T. Farrelly

Superintendent **John T. Farrelly** is Press Relations Officer of the Garda Síochána, based at Garda Headquarters in the Phoenix Park, Dublin. He is the official spokesman for the force, dealing with the media in times of crisis and with all public affairs. John has worked in this department for seven years. Prior to that he was an officer based in Dublin and Donegal. He is a member of the International Security Organisation and the Police Press Officers Europe. John is PR officer for Coiste Siamsa and editor of the Garda Síochána Annual Report. He has two daughters, Stephanie and Michelle. John enjoys fishing, walking and general outdoor activities.

What's in a day?
'A day is something to look forward to or dread. As Press Relations Officer for the Garda Síochána, a day can change within minutes. A murder, a disaster, or a siege is always just a phone call away. Dealing with these awful situations makes you appreciate the good times more, and handle the bad times more easily. We should always appreciate life and live for it. Sometime the day will come when we cannot.'

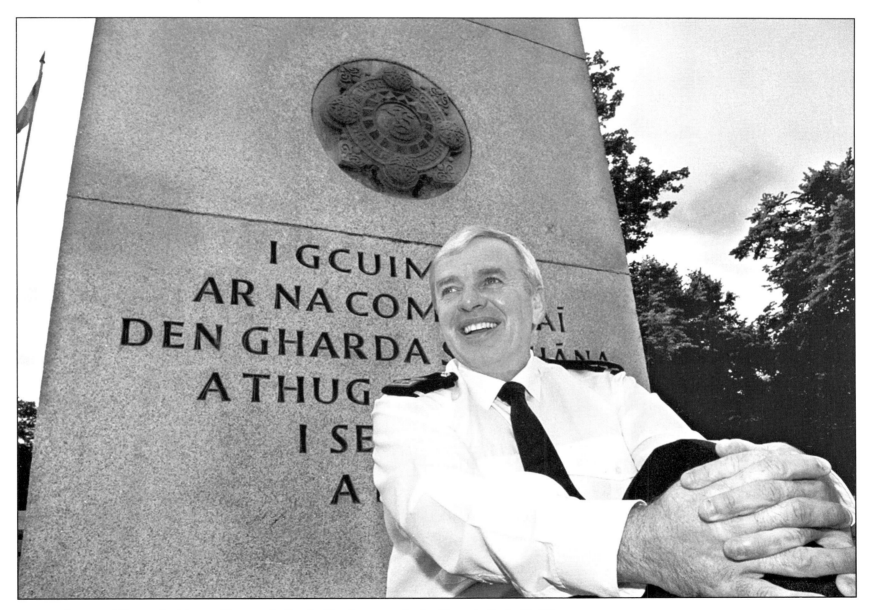

Press Relations Officer John T. Farrelly outside Garda Headquarters in the Phoenix Park, Dublin